DEFENDING HOPE

Dispatches from the front lines in Palestine and Israel
Edited by Eóin Murray and James Mehigan

VERITAS

This book is dedicated to
Iris O'Brien
whose passionate support for human rights in the Middle East, and globally, continues to be an inspiration.

Published 2018 by Veritas Publications
7–8 Lower Abbey Street
Dublin 1, Ireland
publications@veritas.ie
www.veritas.ie

ISBN 978 1 84730 833 7

Copyright © Eóin Murray & James Mehigan

10 9 8 7 6 5 4 3 2 1

The material in this publication is protected by copyright law. Except as may be permitted by law, no part of the material may be reproduced (including by storage in a retrieval system) or transmitted in any form or by any means, adapted, rented or lent without the written permission of the copyright owners. Applications for permissions should be addressed to the publisher.

'End of a Talk with a Jailer' by Samih al Qasim, translated by Nazih Kassis, from *Sadder than Water: New & Selected Poems*, Ibis Editions, 2006. Used with permission.

'Under Siege' by Mahmoud Darwish, from *Unfortunately, It Was Paradise: Selected Poems*, California: University of California Press, 2003. Used with permission.

A catalogue record for this book is available from the British Library.

Cover designed by Lir Mac Cárthaigh, Veritas Publications
Printed in the Republic of Ireland by Watermans Printers Ltd, Cork

Veritas books are printed on paper made from the wood pulp of managed forests. For every tree felled, at least one tree is planted, thereby renewing natural resources.

Contents

Foreword | Mairead Maguire	7
About the Contributors	11
Acknowledgements	15
Introduction	17
A Note on Translation, Transcription and Language	23
Timeline of Major Historical Events Mentioned	25

///

Under Siege | Eóin Murray	29
The Drinking Fountain at the Checkpoint | Jessica Montell	47
Fragmented Hope | Nasser Alissa (Attalah)	67
The Little Acts that Tip the Scales | Arik Ascherman	91
The Power of the Powerless | Ghada Ageel	115
This Life Goes Out to the World Through Our Lenses | Joanne O'Brien	135
High Hopes | Angela Godfrey-Goldstein	171
Planting the Seeds of Home | Lubnah Shomali	187

The Long-Distance Run to Freedom | Sari Bashi   201
To See the Sun Rise Again | Raji Sourani   211

///

Afterword | Andrew Anderson   235
Further Reading and Resources   239

Foreword

It is with profound humility, and deep admiration for the writers involved, that I give this foreword to the book, *Defending Hope: Dispatches from the front lines in Palestine and Israel*.

In 2007 I had the pleasure of meeting Dr Mona el Farra during a visit to Belfast with Trócaire to commemorate the fortieth anniversary of Israel's occupation of the West Bank, East Jerusalem and Gaza Strip. Doctor el Farra is a medical doctor who has spent her life practising in the Gaza Strip. She works with numerous human rights and humanitarian agencies in defence of children and other vulnerable people inside Gaza. Through her blog 'From Gaza with Love' she has become a leading voice on behalf of peace, justice and women's rights.

During her visit, Dr Mona shared with us the story of Gaza and its besieged people. She recounted the agony of life under military occupation. She spoke about the daily bombardments and missiles. She described how the inability to travel freely in or out of Gaza has a particular impact on the sick, who often cannot access medical treatment in Gaza. As a medical doctor, her great concern was the effect this violence was having on Gaza's children who were afraid to sleep at night in fear of being attacked by Israeli drones. These children stand defenceless in the face of Israel's overwhelming military power, whose weapons have been used in Gaza in three recent wars. I was deeply struck by her concluding words: 'Every single person in Gaza is completely traumatised by so much violence and war.'

DEFENDING HOPE

Following Dr Mona's visit to Belfast, I found myself deeply drawn to visit this Holy Land. I travelled with the belief that peace is possible and can be achieved through dialogue and negotiation. However, such a negotiated settlement must be built on a serious desire by the government of Israel to choose peace and non-violence. Peace will only be possible when the military occupation of Palestinian lands comes to an end and Palestinians live with dignity and human rights.

Doctor Mona also came to Belfast to speak about the importance of United Nations Security Council Resolution 1325, which details the particular risks women face during war and also the important role they play in building peace. In my many journeys to the Holy Land (including by boat to Gaza) it has been a joy to march alongside Palestinian women human rights defenders and peacemakers as they resist injustice, including in support of their non-violent campaign for boycott, divestment and sanctions (BDS).

It is now eleven years since Dr Mona visited Belfast. We commemorate fifty-one years of military occupation. It is seventy years since the foundation of the state of Israel, an event known to Palestinians as the Nakba (catastrophe), spawning a refugee crisis that has resulted in generations of cruelty, injustice and pain throughout the wider Middle East.

International law was developed as a way for people, and countries, of conscience the world over to stand against war, apartheid and crimes against humanity. The international community is quick to condemn such acts when they happen in certain other parts of the world; but, despite the awareness of Israel's actions, little has changed for ordinary Palestinians. They

Foreword

do not have a country to call their own, a homeland. Family homes are demolished every day, farms are razed and olive trees uprooted to accommodate the construction of settlements. Different laws apply to Jews and Palestinians who live only kilometres apart. Identity cards are used to determine who can travel, when and to what destination. Little wonder I have encountered South African activists who say what is happening to Palestinians today outweighs many of the most egregious crimes of the regime in their country.

Yet, out of such deep violence and conflict, Palestinian and Israeli peacemakers take a stand in the name of humanity. It is not easy to break the silence or to speak truth to power about injustice. To do so is often to put your life and livelihood at risk.

It makes me profoundly grateful that, during numerous journeys to the region, I have been blessed to meet so many of these deeply inspirational people. The Arabic word *samoud* means perseverance – it is the philosophy by which these peacemakers live. This is deeply meaningful to me because it confirms my view that peace is possible and, because of their efforts, will happen.

These essays are voices of conscience which remind us that, in spite of so much suffering, the darkness is often pierced by the light of courageous Palestinian and Israeli human rights defenders. We take hope when we hear the voices of these extraordinary people. We can be inspired by the stories told in this book and thankful that the contributors chose to bear witness. Above all, we can each pledge to do something to create peace for our Palestinian and Israeli sisters and brothers.

Mairead Maguire
Nobel Peace Laureate

About the Contributors

Ghada Ageel is Visiting Professor of Politics at the University of Alberta. Originally from Khan Younis, in the Gaza Strip, her most recent book is a collection of essays entitled *Apartheid in Palestine: Hard Laws and Harder Experiences*. She writes a regular opinion column for Middle East Eye.

Nasser Alissa (Atallah) is from Deheisheh refugee camp, Bethlehem, OPT. He is the Middle East and North Africa Regional Director with Child Rights International Network (CRIN). The scope of his work at CRIN is tackling child rights violations issues in the region including children in armed conflict, child soldiers, inhuman sentencing and children in conflict with the law. He is the co-founder and Chair of Shoruq Organization which works with refugee children in Palestine.

Andrew Anderson (@ettrick49) is the Executive Director of Front Line Defenders.

Arik Ascherman (@RavArik) is the Director of Torah Tzedek (Torah of Justice), an Israeli NGO. Until 2016 he was President and Chief Rabbi of Rabbis for Human Rights. He is a prominent Jewish activist with relationships in the UK, USA and Canada. He writes a weekly blog for the *Times of Israel*.

Sari Bashi (@saribashi) is the Middle East Director for Human Rights Watch. She was the co-founder of Gisha, the Israeli human rights organisation for freedom of movement.

DEFENDING **HOPE**

Angela Godfrey-Goldstein (@AngelaJerusalem) is the Director of the Jahalin Bedouin Rights Association. She has worked for Israeli human rights organisations for over twenty years and is a regular speaker at Palestinian solidarity conferences in Europe.

Eóin Murray (@eoinmurray) is an Irish activist based in Edmonton, Alberta. He has worked in the non-profit sector in Ireland, the Middle East and Canada since 2003.

James Mehigan (@JamesMehigan) is a human rights barrister at Garden Court Chambers. He lectures in criminology at the Open University. He is a specialist in international criminal and human rights law. He has represented human rights victims and monitored trials internationally. He recently represented families of the victims of the Hillsborough Stadium Disaster.

Jessica Montell (@JessicaMontell) is the Director of Hamoked – Centre for the Defence of the Individual. Until 2015 she was the Director of B'Tselem, Israel's largest human rights organisation. She has been widely published in the international media including in the *Guardian*, *New York Times* and *OpenDemocracy*.

Joanne O'Brien is an Irish photojournalist based in London. She was a founder member of Format, the first all-women photo agency in the UK and she has contributed to *The Irish Times*, the *Guardian* and *The Independent*. She has worked in China, the USA and Europe, and her work is held in the UK's National Portrait Gallery collection. She is the author of two books, *Across*

About the Contributors

the Water about the lives of women in Britain and *A Matter of Minutes* on Bloody Sunday.

Lubnah Shomali (@BADIL_Center) is the Finance and Administration Manager for BADIL Resource Center for Palestinian Residency and Refugee Rights in Bethlehem. Previously she worked with Beit Sahour Municipality as their International Relations Officer. She holds a bachelor's degree in Molecular Biology and a Masters of Business Administration from the University of Michigan.

Raji Sourani (@RajiSourani) is the Director of the Palestinian Centre for Human Rights. In 2015 he was the recipient of the Right Livelihood Award (alternative Nobel Prize). He has also been awarded the RFK Award and the French Republic Award for Human Rights. He is a jurist with the International Commission of Jurists, a board member at FIDH and served as President of the Arab Organisation for Human Rights during the early years of the Arab Spring.

Acknowledgements

When it comes to such a publication there are many hands involved.

Most of all we are grateful to each of the contributors who worked hard to complete pieces when there were many other pressing issues in their lives. We are grateful also to their families and to their employers who allowed them the time to undertake this journey.

As well as her essay on photography, Joanne O'Brien supported the development of the concept and the early editorial phases of the text. She also edited the photograph section, which includes some of her own photographs.

We are grateful to the Iris O'Brien Foundation whose financial support made this project possible.

The team in Veritas Publications who brought the book to fruition have been dedicated and helpful. A special note of thanks goes to Peter O'Connell of TrueLit Publishing Agency who brought us over the finish line in more ways than one.

Andrew Anderson, Noeline Blackwell, the late Frank Jennings and Mary Lawlor from Front Line Defenders have been guiding lights in our lives for many years, not least throughout this piece of work.

A number of people offered professional input, expertise and advice on various elements of the book. These include: Kimmy Beach, Ted Bishop, Richard Crowley, Sybil Cock, Tyler Enfield, Geoffrey Frosh, Jane Mackelworth, Daragh Murray, Tony

DEFENDING HOPE

Murray, John Simms, Marcus Tanner and Veronica Yates. Thank you all for helping us sharpen the tools of the craft.

A large group of dedicated family members and friends offered support in so many areas, over such a long time – more than they can really understand. Thank you to: Abdelhalim, Aidan, Aimie, Alan, Alan, Andrina, Brooke, Dunya, Hamdi, Iyad, Ibetesam, Jane, Janelle, Jaber, Jehan, John, Julie, Khalil, Leigh Ann, Maria, Marina, Mary-Ellen, Mike, Niall, Netta, Noelle, Sabri, Tamarah. Your support was inspirational and essential.

Most of all thank you to our patient and loving families: Natalie, Tom and Hugo; and Isabelle, Max and Ferris. Thank you also to our parents Joe and Patricia, Denis and Mairead. We owe it all to all of you.

Sadly, the project was bookended by the death of two dear friends, pillars in the Palestinian human rights community: Dr Eyad al Sarraj and Bassam al Aqra, both true defenders of hope who are truly missed.

Thank you one and all: many hands made light work.

Eóin Murray & James Mehigan

Introduction

Across the Middle East common wisdom holds that societal change will happen after the pyramids move. The human rights defenders who contributed to this book wake up each day hoping that it will be the one where the ground shifts. But each morning they find the world much as it was the day before: the wall still stands, the checkpoints are still in place and the prospects for peace have not moved any closer. The pyramids have not moved; if anything, they seem even more entrenched than ever.

Both Palestinian and Israeli human rights defenders walk a thin line between hope and despair. For Palestinians hope can sometimes be hard to discern as their society disintegrates under the burden of generations of military occupation and dispossession. For the Israeli contributors to this book – people of conscience who disagree with their government's policies towards Palestinians – daily life may be materially better than their Palestinian counterparts, but their society is legally, morally and spiritually bankrupt.

Despite the challenges each face they continue to work for an end to violence and towards a just and lasting peace. They do this not because they see the horizon but rather because they do not see it, yet know it exists. They choose to act because they carry a common sense of hope. Hope is not the solution, nor the end goal: it is just the beginning.

/ / /

DEFENDING **HOPE**

A human rights defender is anyone who works non-violently for any or all of the rights contained in the Universal Declaration of Human Rights. This may include journalists reporting on demonstrations, ambulance drivers saving lives in a war zone or lawyers bringing cases to court.

Many of those who work to protect human rights do not consider themselves to be human rights defenders. While being subject to the vicissitudes of their own professions or focused on the violations committed against members of their community, they forget the risks that they are taking and the violations of their own rights. However, without the human rights defender – regardless of how they conceive of themselves – there will be nobody to speak truth to power on behalf of the most vulnerable in society.

Recognising this, in 1998, the United Nations General Assembly adopted resolution 53/144, *United Nations Declaration on the Right and Responsibility of Individuals, Groups and Organs of Society to Promote and Protect Universally Recognised Human Rights and Fundamental Freedoms*, which became known as the Declaration on Human Rights Defenders. The declaration recognises 'the right and responsibility of individuals, groups and associations to promote respect for and foster knowledge of human rights and fundamental freedoms at the national and international levels'.

In support of the declaration, a mandate on the situation of human rights defenders was implemented in 2000 and a Special Representative to the Secretary General on the situation of human rights defenders was appointed. Today the position is held by Michel Forst.

Introduction

The situation for human rights defenders around the globe remains a dangerous one. In his 2017 report to the Human Rights Commission, Michel Forst states that 'the Special Rapporteur is more appalled than ever to see attacks against them [human rights defenders] multiplying everywhere, assailing bloggers, indigenous peoples, journalists, community leaders, whistle-blowers and community volunteers'. He sees this as part of a larger global trend not comprised of isolated incidents but a concerted effort to undermine the work of those trying to maintain respect for the Universal Declaration of Human Rights.

The Special Rapporteur's criticisms apply to countries across the world and many of them have refused to engage with his work or allow him to enter their country in an official capacity. At the time of his 2017 report, he had written to the governments of Israel and Palestine requesting an invitation for an official visit. At the time of writing, these invitations had not been forthcoming.

The challenges faced by human rights defenders working in Israel and Palestine are not unique globally and they are certainly not unique within the wider Middle East. Israel is correct to point out that many other countries in the region – and beyond – engage in human rights violations on an egregious scale. The position of the Israeli government is that it deserves different treatment to Iran, Syria or Saudi Arabia because it is the only democracy in the Middle East.

But political leaders such as Jimmy Carter and John Kerry have both warned that Israel is bordering on becoming an apartheid state; many Palestinians feel that this has long been the case. Kerry has taken his remarks further, arguing that Israel can be either Jewish or democratic but it 'cannot be both'.[1]

DEFENDING HOPE

For mainstream American leaders to embrace what were once considered fringe positions is an indication of the success of human rights defenders. When Kerry and Carter speak in this way they are reflecting a range of factors: that the Israeli occupation of Palestinian lands is the longest occupation since the start of the twentieth century; that Israel is one of only two states in the whole world which argues that torture is sometimes justified; that applying different laws to different peoples depending on ethnicity is a form of legal discrimination; that the construction of settlements, the wall, checkpoints and roads only for use by Israelis are all illegal under international law and are creating a situation where a two-state solution is a fiction.

The basis for understanding all of these factors is rooted in the painstaking work of human rights defenders to document every violation, to record the statement of every victim and to noisily advocate for justice and peace.

Because of this success in shifting political discourse, tolerance of dissent by Israeli human rights defenders is at a nadir since the foundation of the Jewish state. Attacks on individuals and institutions trying to uphold values of dignity and equality have intensified.

Likewise, within the Palestinian Authority, there are also many attacks on human rights defenders as they document crackdowns by police on demonstrations or record the torture inflicted inside Palestinian jails. The still unhealed division in political control between the West Bank and the Gaza Strip has done little to bolster the rights of citizens in either area. Human rights defenders criticising the government – whether in Gaza or Ramallah – have been arrested, beaten and threatened.

Introduction

Such attacks, wherever they come from, seek to undermine the values of democracy and create the conditions for tyranny. But human rights defenders come to see the value in them too; as Rabbi Arik Ascherman remarks in his essay, there's nothing quite as good for solidarity as 'getting beaten up together'.

Struggling on an additional front are those female human rights defenders who face additional stigma by virtue of the fact that they are women. Toxic masculinity is almost the defining feature of Palestinian and Israeli social paradigms, so women face extra burdens as they document and report on injustice.

One example is that of Samar Abu Elouf who, while documenting the 2014 Gaza war, was mocked by men who asked her 'what's for dinner?' Sexist attitudes near home also translate into struggles to access resources for her work from abroad. Perhaps because of this experience of multiple levels of discrimination it is often female human rights defenders who draw the clearest links between struggles for justice, which may initially appear to be at the margins of the conflict: housing rights, LGBTQ rights, women's rights and anti-racist work all form part of a wider struggle against oppressive systems.

/ / /

The human rights defenders in this book sometimes have to struggle to do something as simple as get to their place of work safely. When they do they face the very real possibility that their office will be burned down or blown up. They live in a world which no longer prioritises their right to life or the suffering in their region. There are too many other things wrong with the world for the rights of Palestinians to be a priority.

This book seeks to refocus attention on the lives and remarkable work of fourteen Palestinian and Israeli human rights defenders. Given the barriers of language and resources our selection of contributors aimed, as much as possible, to achieve a balanced representation between women and men, and also between Palestinians and Israelis. As editors we have included four Palestinian, four Israeli and two international contributors. As interview subjects (in the essay about photo-journalism) we include a further Israeli, an international voice and four Palestinian voices. All the contributors gave liberally of their time and expertise – for which we are very grateful.

If we ignore their suffering and their courage for another generation then we risk extinguishing the light of hope – leaving despair as their only option. Keeping hope alive is as much our responsibility as theirs.

Eóin Murray & James Mehigan
Edmonton & London, 2018

Note

1. John Kerry, Secretary of State, 'Remarks on Middle East Peace', at the Dean Acheson Auditorium in Washington D.C., 28 December 2016. 2009-2017.state.gov/secretary/remarks/2016/12/266119.htm.

A Note on Translation, Transcription and Language

Arabic and Hebrew are the primary languages spoken in the Middle East. Neither use the Latin script and sometimes sounds prevalent in both languages cannot be easily transferred to the English language.

We have chosen to standardise formats of common words used throughout the text with an emphasis on readability and ease of pronunciation, rather than on linguistic precision. Most of the Arabic and Hebrew words or phrases used in the text are proper nouns so we have opted, in those cases, not to italicise them. Common examples include Nakba and intifada. Other phrases have been included in italics.

A more complex decision lies in the area of English language phrases which describe the same object, but from different perspectives. A simple example of this is found in the case of the 'Apartheid Wall' versus the 'Security Barrier'. In such instances we have decided against editorial intervention, instead allowing the contributor to choose their own terminology, supposing that it rests with them to persuade the reader of the most appropriate language to describe contentious subject matter.

This may pose occasional problems for readers as they struggle to identify if certain objects referred to in one piece are the same as those referred to in another piece. In such cases we encourage you to plough on regardless and let the contributor guide you into the world they have created and the language they choose to use in creating that world.

Timeline of Major Historical Events Mentioned

1917 – British occupy Palestine: As World War I draws to an end the British forces take control of Palestine from the Ottoman Empire. The British assume control, under the authority of the League of Nations, as a 'Mandatory Power'. British Foreign Secretary Arthur Balfour signs a secret declaration committing British support for the establishment of a Jewish 'national homeland' in Palestine.

1945 – The Holocaust: As World War II comes to a close, Allied forces liberate concentration camps designed for the slaughter of Jews, Roma, LGBTQ and other minority groups. At least six million Jews were killed in the Holocaust.

1948 – Establishment of the state of Israel: 15 May marks Israeli Independence Day. It took just a matter of minutes for the USA to recognise the new state and other states quickly followed suit. Arab states attacked the newly formed state and the first Arab-Israeli war took place.

1948 – Palestinian Nakba occurs: Seven hundred and fifty thousand Palestinians are driven from their homes and villages and over four hundred villages are completely destroyed. The Palestinians live as refugees in neighbouring states (Syria, Jordan, Egypt and Lebanon) but many move to the West Bank and the Gaza Strip. Israel's Law of Return prevents them from coming back to their country. United Nations General Assembly resolution 194/48 bestows on the refugees an inheritable and inalienable right of return.

1949 – Fourth Geneva Convention signed: On 12 August 1949 the Fourth Geneva Convention Relative to the Protection of Civilians in Wartime was signed. It followed from the other Geneva Conventions and the creation of the Universal Declaration of Human Rights in 1948.

1967 – Israel wins the Six-Day War: Israel launches a 'pre-emptive' strike against Egypt, Syria and Jordan. UN Resolution 242 calls for Israeli withdrawal from 'territories occupied'. On 29 June, Israel annexed East Jerusalem, arguing that Jerusalem is Israel's 'eternal, undivided capital'.

1973 – Yom Kippur/Ramadan War: Egypt and Syria launch a surprise attack against Israel during the holy time of Yom Kippur (the Jewish Day of Repentance) and in the middle of the Muslim fasting period of Ramadan. Israel wins the war.

1987 – First Intifada: The first Palestinian intifada begins in Jabaliya refugee camp in northern Gaza.

1993 – Oslo Accords signed: Following secret talks between the Palestinian Liberation Organisation (PLO) and Israel a 'Declaration of Principles' is signed in Oslo, establishing Palestinian autonomy in certain parts of the Occupied Palestinian Territory (OPT) (but not East Jerusalem), joint Palestinian-Israeli security control in some areas and full Israeli control in others. Israel agrees to end settlement expansion and the PLO

Timeline of Major Historical Events Mentioned

recognises the State of Israel. The Palestinian Authority is the by-product of the agreement and takes control over the areas of Palestinian autonomy, while the PLO remains the international representative of the Palestinian people.

1994 – Ibrahimi Mosque massacre: On 25 February 1994 an Israeli settler, Baruch Goldstein, kills twenty-nine Palestinian civilians and wounds one hundred and twenty-five others when he opens fire with a machine gun inside the Ibrahimi Mosque, a site sacred to the Abrahamic faiths, in Hebron.

1994 – First 'suicide attack' in Tel Aviv: The 'Islamic Resistance Movement' (Hamas) blows up a bus in Tel Aviv, the first time such an attack had happened in the city. Twenty-two Israelis died and fifty were injured.

1995 – Yitzhak Rabin killed: An Israeli settler, Yigal Amir, assassinated Yitzhak Rabin for his part in signing the Oslo Accords.

2000 – Second Intifada: The second Palestinian intifada begins.

2005 – Israel 'disengages' from Gaza: Israel removes its settlements from the Gaza Strip but retains effective control over air, sea and land access to the Strip.

2006/7 - Hamas/Fatah split: Hamas beat Fatah in Palestinian elections, resulting in an international and Israeli boycott of the new government. Rising tensions led to violent clashes between the two parties in Gaza, resulting in serious civilian casualties and a split in Palestinian governance between the West Bank and Gaza Strip. Despite reconciliation efforts Gaza remains under de facto Hamas control and the West Bank is run by Fatah through the Palestinian Authority.

2008/9 – Israeli war on Gaza known as Operation Cast Lead: On 26 December 2008 Israel launched a twenty-three-day war on the Gaza Strip.

2012 – Israeli war on Gaza known as Operation Pillar of Defence: Israel launches an eight-day offensive on the Gaza Strip.

2012 – Palestinian Statehood at the UN: The UN General Assembly passed a resolution granting the State of Palestine non-member observer status, an upgrade which allowed the Palestinians to enter UN bodies, including to ask the International Criminal Court to investigate war crimes during the wars in Gaza.

2014 – Israeli war on Gaza known as Operation Protective Edge: Israel launches fifty-one day offensive on Gaza.

2017 – US embassy to move to Jerusalem: US President Donald Trump announces that his country's embassy will move from Tel Aviv to Jerusalem. The move is welcomed by Israel but condemned by most of the rest of the world in a vote at the UN General Assembly.

Under Siege

Eóin Murray

Here on the slopes of hills, facing the dusk and
the cannon of time
Close to the gardens of broken shadows,
We do what prisoners do,
And what the jobless do:
We cultivate hope.
 – *from 'Under Siege' by Mahmoud Darwish*

Morning prayer ends. A missile splits the pre-dawn sky. I spring awake in bed. Throwing on a dressing gown and slippers, I walk cautiously out of my apartment. The street quiet, the palm-trees still, on a balcony above I see two women weeping. Afraid to go wandering in these unknown streets, uncertain as to what might be around the next corner, I hear the distant din of a crowd gathering. Sirens play against the sky like off-key piano notes. My curiosity pushes me forward but my fear holds me back. I advance two blocks with all the grace of a clumsy spy, peering around each corner lest I find an angry mob waiting for me. At each corner there is nothing and no one, just parked cars, and the kind of quiet found in late night suburbia. I cannot locate the centre of the noise so decide to return home where I tune my radio to the BBC World Service, hoping for information about what has just taken place. It is my first night in the Gaza Strip, the welcome is as noisy as I expected.

DEFENDING **HOPE**

When people hear I lived in Gaza their response is usually one of bewilderment – why on earth would anyone want to go there? It's a fair question. During my time there, Gaza was awarded the dubious honour of being the most dangerous place on earth. The name itself is an easy byword for human suffering. As one of Gaza's pre-eminent chroniclers, the Israeli journalist Amira Hass, tells us, in Hebrew to say 'Go to Gaza' is the idiomatic equivalent of 'Go to Hell'. For most people their perception of Gaza matches the description given by Dante as he passes in to hell 'through the gate to a strange land, Where sighs and moans and screams of ruined men, Filling the air beneath a starless sky, Resounded everywhere.'[1]

There is some substance to this perception. The Gaza Strip is as long as a marathon and approximately one third as wide. The Strip's tiny area is in inverse proportion to the tumultuous waves it creates in the global political landscape. The intense poverty, the seemingly insoluble conflict supported by the news pictures of angry, bearded men shouting 'Allahu akhbar' as they carry yet another muslin-wrapped corpse through the streets. It all constructs an image of a place that is unstable and unattractive. Yet, for me, moving to Gaza was an easy decision. An opportunity arose to work for a Palestinian human rights organisation headquartered in the Gaza Strip. It was a well-established institution with a reputation for fearless critiques of the Israeli military as well as the Palestinian Authority. I had always been looking for such an opportunity. Growing up, the conflict in Northern Ireland was formative in my political psyche but, being from Dublin, I was privileged not to experience it directly.

Under Siege

Of course there were many places where injustice lived. Chance, and helpful friends, both played a part in ensuring I ended up in Gaza. But there was more. The intensity of debate over the Middle East made it worthy of independent discovery. Gaza offered a mystery to solve: a mystery blended by a combination of religion, history and politics offered almost nowhere else. What, I wondered, was really happening? On the one hand I held an activist's visceral sense of an injustice being visited upon Palestinians. On the other hand I carried inside the quietly spoken words of a close Jewish colleague who asked me to always remember that there were, indeed, two sides to every story.

The man killed in the pre-dawn explosion was Sheikh Ahmad Yassin, the spiritual leader of Hamas. The women sobbing on the balcony that morning were probably already aware of who had been killed, or perhaps they simply sobbed for another Gaza bombing. Either way their tears were not the last shed in Gaza. Nor was Yassin's blood the first, or the last, to fall on this troubled stretch of land.

///

If you stand at night-time on the beach in Gaza City and look north your eyes will see the industrial towers and lights of the Israeli ports of Ashkelon and Ashdod. Just a few hours further north is Tel Aviv, then Haifa, and so the road – if accessible – would lead all the way to Beruit. Face south and the land curves gently – follow the southern road, and you would find yourself in the Sinai desert.

DEFENDING **HOPE**

For an army travelling north from the Sinai, Gaza was the first place to encounter water after a desert trek. For an army heading south into Egypt, Gaza was the last place to stock up on supplies. Gaza is a crossroads of ancient and strategic significance. Its stories have entered popular mythology – not least among them the tale of Samson and Delilah. But other stories, too.

As he travelled down the coast from modern Lebanon, Alexander the Great terrorised the local populations by stringing together a long, human necklace of crucifixes from Tyre to Ashdod. His message was clear: resist me as they did in Tyre and you will receive this punishment. All the populations capitulated immediately, until Alexander reached Gaza. The city refused to submit and in 332 BC Alexander laid siege. He anticipated a fairly easy win. In the end, it took Alexander one hundred days to overcome the besieged city. Alexander was brutal in victory: he killed all those suspected of fighting and sold their families as slaves.

For Gazans, siege warfare is an integral part of the city's history. The Bible records that a little over one hundred and fifty years after Alexander's attack came the siege of the Maccabees who also conquered Gaza. Over the course of the twentieth century no less than four major powers controlled the Strip: the Ottomans, the British, the Egyptians and the Israelis. My time in Gaza was during the most modern incarnation of the siege.

The contemporary siege on Gaza has a number of distinct phases. The earliest phase runs, roughly, from 1948 up to 1967. The population of Gaza was largely displaced refugees, catered to by the United Nations in Egyptian controlled territory. However, the refugee population was forbidden from returning

Under Siege

to live in their previous homes in the newly minted State of Israel. Visitations were sometimes permitted. Many friends in Gaza remember their experience as children being taken by their grandparents to see the old village. Their grandparents would look for familiar landmarks like their home or the well where the women drew water. But most of the landmarks had been erased. The old villages were lost. After recounting their story they would point at the wall in the dwelling in the refugee camp where we sat. Hanging in a frame would be the cast-iron key to the old family home. The key hung as a reminder for all that was lost through the passage of history but, with patience, all that might be regained through the passage of time.

The next phase of the Gaza siege runs from the beginning of Israel's military occupation in 1967 through the first Palestinian uprising and into the period of the Oslo Accords in the 1990s. The siege had its variations but in essence limited travel was permitted. Between 1967 and 1972 Gaza was declared a closed military zone – access was only possible based on permission from the local military commander. After 1972 this prohibition was lifted in relation to travel to Israel and the West Bank (but not for international travel). A series of military checkpoints controlled access in and out of the Strip. Many of my Israeli friends recall their families taking them on day trips to the beach and to Gaza's bustling markets. Palestinians recall visiting friends in Jerusalem, Haifa or Tel Aviv. While there was surely a significant degree of mutual antipathy, the possibility of human connection still existed. Even though a period of peace was emerging at the political level the possibilities for human connection between Gazans and Israelis were made more difficult in the early and mid 1990s when Gaza residents were required to get permits to travel to Israel. The subsequent breakdown of trust at the local and political levels during the Oslo period would have serious consequences for the Palestinian residents of Gaza.

By the end of the millennium Israeli society was scarred and embittered by attacks on citizens standing in bars or at bus stops. Palestinians were beleaguered by shootings, arrests and destruction of land and livelihoods. The second intifada began in September 2000 sparking a dramatic escalation in the level of military conflict and a sharp tightening of the travel restrictions on people living inside the Gaza Strip.

Israel began to construct a concrete wall around Gaza. Military checkpoints turned into watchtowers. Gaza's only airport, near the Egyptian border, was destroyed. The Oslo Accords set a twelve-nautical mile limit on Palestinian control of the sea. But Gaza's fishermen often found themselves sailing only four or five nautical miles before meeting a gunboat from the Israeli navy who would fire warnings to encourage them back towards the shore.

One of the curiosities of the siege on Gaza during the second intifada was how it operated as a Russian doll: a siege, within a siege, within a siege. Around eight thousand Israeli settlers lived in towns throughout the Strip. These areas controlled around 45 per cent of Gaza's landmass. To protect these settlers and settlements, the army constructed military installations inside the Strip itself. The most famous among these was at Abu Houli checkpoint. By closing the road here the army could cut the Strip in half, so preventing Palestinians from moving from one end of the Strip to the other.

Under Siege

Then, within this already truncated piece of land were situated other smaller enclaves. Near the southern town of Khan Younis existed a small village called al Mawasi, a strip of land one kilometre wide and fourteen kilometres long running along Gaza's coastline. Underneath al Mawasi lies a large water table which provides excellent water for use in agriculture. To the east the village was entirely surrounded by the settlements known as Gush Qatif. As far back as 1982 the five thousand or so residents of al Mawasi faced more serious movement restrictions than other residents of the Strip. But after the killing of an Israeli settler by an al Mawasi resident in 2001 the restrictions intensified. Residents were issued special ID cards which allowed only them to access the village. Movement, in and out, was controlled through al Tufah (the Apple) checkpoint – a heavily armoured access point operating between 8 a.m. and 4 p.m.

The first time I stood outside the checkpoint at al Mawasi groups of women and children exited with empty shopping bags going to get food supplies for the week. They walked with stooped heads, carrying a fearful weight upon their shoulders. (Women did not leave their children behind inside al Mawasi lest they return to find the checkpoint closed. It might not open again until the next day, or the next week.) An oppressive silence followed these bowed-headed women, none of the noise and excitement that a trip to market might otherwise engender. Instead there was an absence of presence, the kind of fearful shyness characteristic of someone who is subject to regular bouts of violent abuse.

For those who did not live inside enclaves like al Mawasi, life was still deeply unpredictable. Access to the outside world was solely done through the Rafah crossing point into Egypt. In 2004 the crossing point was closed for over two months. Even when it opened, movement was forbidden for men and women between the ages of sixteen and thirty-five. This particularly impacted those who had won scholarships or who had secured student visas and were ready to travel to university in the Gulf, Europe or the USA.

Siege, in and of itself, is not forbidden by international law. But components of how a siege is often fought, can be. Anything targeting or punishing the civilian population is forbidden and considered a war crime. Michael Walzer, a moral philosopher who has considered the justifications for warfare, views siege as 'the oldest form of warfare'. Gaza's history bears this out and Walzer highlights 'the goal is surrender ... [t]he means is not the defeat of the enemy army, but the fearful spectacle of the civilian dead.'[2] By drip-feeding access of humanitarian supplies, including medicine and food, Israel found a way to keep the people of the Gaza Strip on a life support machine. The goal was to starve the population just enough to create a reaction against the ruling party – once Fatah, now Hamas. Almost a fifth of a century after this strategy was first instigated, no such reaction has occurred.

/ / /

There's no McDonalds in Gaza. But there are plenty of locally run fast-food outlets serving Western fare. There is also ample competition from the falafel vendors on the streets packing locally grown vegetables and spiced chickpeas into the local pita, which is baked with wholewheat. Corner stores selling supplies

Under Siege

often have full shelves. In 2004 and 2005 tunnels for smuggling goods were not as sophisticated as they later became – but they did exist and any goods in short supply from the siege were easily brought in through these tunnels. For most Gazans anything beyond the staples of flour and chickpeas are hard to afford but lack of money does not equate to lack of availability.

The siege was also hard to detect at the tables of Gaza's many wonderful restaurants. Close observers of their dishes might notice that, over time, the size of the prawns served in the traditional *zibdiya* (shrimp baked in spicy tomato sauce) shrunk because the fishermen cannot travel far enough out to sea. Consequently, they over-fish the areas close to the shore where the prawns reproduce, catching younger and smaller prawns. Over time, the thirty thousand people who work in Gaza's fishing industry will have no choice but to deplete their stock to the point where it is non-existent.

But the siege is easy to find on the faces of almost every citizen of the Strip. The late Dr Eyad al Sarraj, a leader of Gaza's civil society movement, used to say that almost every Gazan carries trauma within. They wear it in their eyes. Yet, how Gazans respond to the trauma of siege varies.

Watching the women at al Mawasi, it becomes apparent that the siege takes form in a person's inner life. The mindset of siege is that of shrinking so as not to be noticed, of closing down to the pain of the external reality where every move and gesture has to be considered lest it cause offence.

There is a felt-sense of shame in being oppressed. The self-blame is very real – people ask themselves 'why me?', 'why us?', 'what did I do in this life, or a previous one, to deserve this treatment?'

DEFENDING HOPE

All these questions have no obvious answer. The shame of being unable to provide a home, or a meal for one's family, is a kind of solitary confinement. Many people suffer in silence, uncertain of how to change these circumstances which overwhelm them.

But release from the shame of prison does not rely on a change in external circumstances – rather it happens when we realise that the shame is of our own making, even if the prison is not. Even in the depth of prison there is a chance to conduct oneself with inner freedom. It is often taken as truth that those who have been abused or oppressed have an increased propensity towards inflicting suffering on others weaker than them. But many Gazans, indeed, most Gazans, defy this stereotype.

Early one morning, while accompanying a group of Swedish diplomats on a tour of the Strip, we visited Rafah, an area in the south that was often at the frontline of fighting between the Israeli military and the Palestinian factions. Just a few hours previously the military had withdrawn from a neighbourhood where they were conducting an operation to destroy tunnels. To do this the area had been sealed off by tanks and foot-soldiers so that armoured bulldozers could demolish the houses in the hope of locating any smuggling tunnels underneath them.

It had started around two in the morning. The sound of the army coming alerted residents to the beginning of this mini-siege. Then came the loudhailers warning them to evacuate their homes. Soon afterwards intense lights shone through their windows. One family rushed out of bed, doing a quick headcount on their children and trying to go out the front door. Reaching the front door, they realised that the bulldozer was already approaching so they scrambled to go out the back. The intensity of the noise frightened the children who were panicking and difficult to eject out the window.

We were standing on the rubble of a home as all this was described to us by one of the residents. He was an English teacher in a local school who could speak eloquently about the night's events. Around us were the fragments of his life: papers flapping in the wind, a crushed fridge surrounded by grey concrete blocks with metal poles protruding. Children played in the rubble while nearby a group of women lit a fire and huddled close. The smell of the fire blended with the smell of munitions and gunpowder which hung in the air. Silence surrounded us, heavy with pain, but the kind of silence from which some sort of truth might find the space to emerge.

Everything this man once had was gone: his home, his clothes, family memorabilia, children's toys, his ID cards and paperwork. Hardly anything could be salvaged. Then, about half way through his explanations, a small boy, perhaps eight years old, arrived along with a metal tray. On it were small glasses full of tea, short porcelain cups of cardamom-infused coffee and a small white plate piled with pita bread. The man encouraged us to eat while he continued talking. We stood, stunned by this offer and politely tried to decline. A smile opened up his face and he said, 'You are guests of ours, please eat and drink.'

The generosity of the offer is still hard to imagine. Somewhere from the depths of a destroyed neighbourhood this man's family had found a way to provide the privileged, Western visitors with refreshments. In the end we accepted because the kindness of the offer was so powerful. To accept it was to afford the family a dignity that the destruction of their home did not offer.

DEFENDING **HOPE**

What seemed like a simple gesture demonstrated the human capacity for finding kindness in the darkest of circumstances. No matter the darkness our response is a choice: we can serve tea or become angry.

///

The laws on siege warfare date back to at least the Book of Deuteronomy, though as the example of Alexander the Great shows, they were scarcely observed by attacking armies. Citing the Nuremberg trial of German Field Marshal von Leeb, Michael Walzer argues that if a besieged population is given freedom to leave the area then a much greater latitude for military operations is tolerated under international law. But if civilians remain in the besieged area then the use of starvation and economic warfare is far less acceptable because, as Walzer describes:

> a soldier must take careful aim *at* his military target and away from non-military targets. He can only shoot if he has a reasonably clear shot; he can only attack if a direct attack is possible. He can risk incidental deaths but he cannot kill civilians simply because he finds them between himself and his enemies.[3]

This principle of the laws of warfare has today become so ingrained as to be foundational. It represents the moral, legal and political basis upon which the world has agreed wars ought to be fought, even if, as the siege on Gaza demonstrates, it is often widely ignored.

Under Siege

Although laws of warfare have a long historical precedence in religious and political treatises it was not until after World War II that these laws gained universal favour. The nightmare of the Holocaust, the mass siege on cities like Leningrad and the British blockade of Germany were all fresh in the minds of those who gathered to clean the moral wreckage of the war.

Their efforts became codified in a revolutionary document, one of history's most beautiful creations: the Universal Declaration of Human Rights (UDHR). Just after the UDHR came into force a series of conventions on the laws of war were also given legal status. These were known as the Geneva Conventions.

The international system of moral laws codified in the UDHR and the Geneva Conventions is under heavy attack today from both the left and right. On the right they are perceived as having an overbearing effect on the necessity to implement 'security' measures to protect the general population. On the left they face the accusation of being tools of Western powers, still acting as if they had colonial rights to subjugate the people and resources of foreign lands.

Yet, despite these attacks – and the apparent failures of the system to provide protection for the most vulnerable, in war and peace – here is a system which recognised the rights of 'all human beings in dignity and equality' balancing debates between those who see the world through a prism of individual liberty and those who prefer collective responsibility. This is coupled with a desire to create legal accountability for people who suffer untold horrors.

In many years living and working in the Gaza Strip, observing hundreds of students being trained in the philosophy of human rights, speaking to many hundreds of individuals, I never met

DEFENDING HOPE

one who objected to the idea that they had rights and that those rights ought to be respected. People often despaired at the failure of governments to ensure that their rights were respected. But this reflects the inadequacy of the system to provide justice rather than the idea of justice itself. For all its limitations the human rights philosophy remains a beacon for the powerless.

In 2005 an ex-commander of the Israeli military in the Gaza Strip, Major-General Doron Almog, fled an arrest warrant issued by a judge in Bow Street Magistrates Court, London. Almog refused to disembark from the El Al flight that he had just landed on because he received a tip-off that the Metropolitan Police's War Crimes and Anti-Terrorism Unit were waiting for him. In the immediate aftermath the focus of the media was on the impact of Almog, and others in a similar position, who would board every plane with trepidation of what might await them on the other side.

I spoke to one of the Gazan plaintiffs who had brought the case with the help of Palestinian and British lawyers. With a bittersweet smile he simply offered: 'I feel sorry for him – now he knows for one day what it is like to be a Palestinian every day.' For this man, and the others, who petition international courts for justice, the ideal of human rights is the last refuge of their hopes that justice can be achieved.

/ / /

One of the great shocks any visitor to Gaza receives is how busy and vibrant the place is. To some degree this is a function of space: placing that many people in a small area of land automatically

Under Siege

generates a certain amount of industry. But Gazans also generate an enormous amount of industry because of their circumstances.

The centre of Gaza City is one long, stubborn, traffic jam. Pedestrians walk directly onto the road, the cars inch forward competing to enter the available space and keep moving. Sometimes pedestrians or cars move forward too quickly and then move back from their advance. It is a poorly coordinated set-dance of two million people bumping off each other, just trying to get their daily business done.

Living under siege forces an industrial level of creativity because no task can be taken for granted. In the 2007/8 war Gaza's power plant was bombed by the Israeli Air Force. This bombing came a few weeks after Israel had declared Gaza as a 'hostile foreign entity', so beginning another intense phase of the siege.

The power plant never received the materials required to reconstruct it because the materials were not allowed into Gaza. This, combined with the failings of both the Hamas government and the Palestinian Authority in the West Bank, ensured that electricity remains in short supply across Gaza (which goes some way to explain the endless traffic jams: no functioning traffic lights). The human ingenuity of combatting this is evident when you enter a Gaza home and see elaborate systems of car batteries hooked up to generators running televisions, cookers and mobile phone chargers. In poorer homes cooking is done on open gas stoves. (Al Ahli Hospital is full every day with toddlers being treated for serious burns caused when they bump into a kerosene stove.) For me it all demonstrated that no matter what is directed at people they find the inner energy to resist and to create new ways to go on living.

DEFENDING HOPE

///

If Gaza City is the busiest part of the Strip the most intense source of bustle in the city is the area of Shuja'iyya, Gaza's toughest neighbourhood. It sits close to the eastern border with Israel so is subject to intense and frequent battles. It is also close to the old Ottoman centre of Gaza, home to the ancient mosque and to an old Turkish bathhouse which still functions today.

In 2016 I visited the home of Maha al Sheikh Khalil. Her family home was at the very heart of the 2014 conflict. Maha was six when her family home was destroyed during the war. She was hiding behind a door in the house during heavy shelling in the neighbourhood when a shell landed right on top of the doorway.

Her mother, two sisters and five other family members were killed. Her brother was injured with shrapnel that lodged in his head. To remove it would be unsafe so he suffers chronic pain and serious mental health problems. Her elder sister had the bottom half of her face completely blown off. Her jaw, her teeth and mouth – everything is gone.

And Maha, herself, is tetraplegic as a result of shrapnel entering – then exiting – her neck. The shrapnel caused fractures in the fourth, fifth, sixth and seventh vertebrae, as well as to her spinal column.

We were sitting in the small courtyard in her aunt's home. The area was flat so she could be maneuvered in her wheelchair. The customary tea and coffee sat on the table. Until a few months previously she had lived in the shell of her demolished home with no toilet, no electricity and no facilities to care for her.

Under Siege

I sat listening to her father's words. They were heavy and full of the pain of the responsibilities that he could not fulfill. He had remarried, and recently had a new baby. He found occasional work as a labourer but the family had no regular supply of income to feed the baby, his new wife, Maha's aunt, and Maha's five other sisters and one brother.

Maha needs daily care from a massage therapist but the family cannot afford to provide it. They received no support from the Hamas government who had promised to rebuild their previous home. There was limited support from one or two charitable organisations, and one or two charitable individuals. But nothing sustainable was available. The lack of electricity meant it was hard to heat the home adequately and Maha often endured colds. But her paralysis meant that she could not clear the phlegm from her throat. She cannot swallow. She had just come back from a three day stay in hospital for an operation: the doctors had cut a hole in her throat, inserted a tube then vacuumed out the mucus.

Maha has no way to communicate with words. Most days she goes to Shams al Amal (Sun of Hope) school. This is Gaza's only school for the disabled and was also destroyed during the 2014 war (then later rebuilt). At school Maha paints pictures of extraordinary colour and beauty. As I listened to her dad she watched me playfully. Inside her was a trapped vibrancy. She pushed that untapped energy from every part of her body out through those small areas where she could still move. Her eyes twinkled and when she caught my eye she would close hers, then open them again rapidly, playing hide-and-go-seek. She smiled throughout the entire experience, with her mouth but also with her eyes. She has limited hand movements but they waved and gesticulated as if she was engaged in a carefree dance along the road home after school.

I left the house shortly after to travel out of Gaza, to the Erez checkpoint, uncertain when I might have the chance to return. Maha was born three years after Ahmad Yassin was killed. Over twelve years living, then working, in Gaza she was the smallest of all the Russian dolls I encountered: her body under siege. But, like the rest of Gaza, inside of her was a powerful light, streaming out, searching for the life it knows is there.

Notes

1. Dante Alighieri, *The Divine Comedy*, New York: Liveright Publishing Corporation, 2013 (Kindle Edition), p. 16.
2. Michael Walzer, *Just and Unjust Wars: A Moral Argument with Historical Illustrations*, New York: Basic Books, 1977.
3. Ibid.

The Drinking Fountain at the Checkpoint

Jessica Montell

When my daughter Tal was one year old she got a very high fever. I watched the thermometer climb higher every half hour. I called the doctor in a panic when it reached thirty-nine degrees. 'Put her in the bathtub to bring the fever down,' the doctor told me. 'If she still has a fever, bring her to see me in the morning.'

The next morning her fever was still high. I put her in the car and started driving across Jerusalem to the doctor's office. The whole way, I couldn't get another little girl out of my mind. Ala Ahmed was ten years old and lived about fifty miles from our house. Fifty miles, but light years away. My family lives in West Jerusalem, in liberal, democratic, first-world Israel. Ala's family lives in a village next to Nablus, in the third-world West Bank, which has been under Israeli military occupation since 1967.

This was October 2000, the beginning of the second Palestinian uprising and the Israeli military imposed a siege on towns and villages throughout the West Bank, including Ala's village, preventing anyone from getting in or out. On 13 October, Ala's appendix ruptured and she complained of stomach pains. Her father wanted to take her to Rafidiyeh Hospital, just ten miles down the road in Nablus, but no taxi driver was willing to take them, out of fear of the soldiers. The stomach pains worsened, and she started to vomit. The father then begged his neighbour to drive them to Nablus, and he agreed.

'We put Ala into the car and drove to the main road,' Ala's father recounted. 'An Israeli military vehicle stopped us. "Where are you going?" a soldier asked. "We have a child who needs to get to the hospital," I told him. He said, "Go back quickly and don't say a word; it's forbidden to travel."'

'I tried with all my might to convince him, but without success. The soldier said, "Go home." We tried to go another way, but soldiers stopped us and said that it was forbidden to enter Nablus or to travel. We got home and I called Dr Riad al-Halu from the village nearby. He came and examined Ala and said that it was urgent that she get to a hospital. But Ala remained at home until the next morning. At about 8.30 a.m. I tried again to get Ala to Nablus. We came across another Israeli patrol, who ordered us to go back home. We tried to get her to drink herbal tea, but she wouldn't. When I realised that nothing was helping, and the soldiers wouldn't let us pass, I again took her to Dr Riad, but when we got to his clinic, Ala died and he couldn't do anything.'

Tears come to my eyes every time I think about this father, frantically trying everything as he watches his little girl die before his eyes. Ala was the first victim of Israel's siege policy. She died just a few weeks before I put my daughter Tal in the car for the uneventful drive to our family doctor.

'It looks like a virus,' the doctor reassured me after examining my daughter. 'There's a nasty one going around.' It took me fifteen minutes to get home. No surprises on the way, no delays.

/ / /

We, in Israel, live in a schizophrenic reality: a liberal democracy maintaining a military occupation. It's not a military occupation thousands of miles away, like US forces in Iraq. Here occupation

The Drinking Fountain at the Checkpoint

is right next door. Most Israelis don't see occupation. They go about their lives with no understanding of how our policies affect millions of people who live just down the road. The military's restrictions on movement and the societal polarisation keep most Israelis in their democracy bubble, while most Palestinians are stuck in their occupation bubble. And so the two populations live side by side with little interaction. Certainly, the Jews have little understanding of the Palestinian reality.

A few of us leave our bubble and visit Palestinians. We need no time machine or jet plane. We do not even require a passport to enter a reality so different from our own. I spent over a decade documenting the Israeli occupation, often spending the day in the occupied West Bank and returning home to democratic Israel in time to cook dinner and help my kids with their homework. I would return disoriented, suffering from something akin to jet lag: re-entering life in Israel with images of that parallel universe of occupation running through my head.

It is a privilege to be able to cross between Israeli and Palestinian societies, to meet Palestinians who share my values and to work together to promote those values. It is also a responsibility. Once you know what is happening just over there, you can never un-know it. Human rights work in our context is full of setbacks. I imagine this is true of human rights work all over the world. The work is frustrating. It can feel like we have made no gains, with the situation only getting worse. Precisely because of the frequent setbacks, I believe it is important to recognise and celebrate the achievements.

The checkpoints around Nablus were removed a few years ago. Sick people like little Ala Ahmed are no longer impeded in their access to the hospital. Students can now travel freely to university. People can get to their jobs. Did our work play a role in this change? If so, it is a very partial, even unsatisfying achievement: checkpoints that never should have been installed in the first place have been removed. It reminds me of the well-known Jewish story about a man who turns to his rabbi to complain that his tiny home is crowded, noisy and dirty. The rabbi advises him to bring the family's goat into the house and the man, though confused, complies. The next week the rabbi tells him to bring in some chickens, and then the cow. Finally, when the man can't bear it any more, the rabbi tells him to remove all the animals. The man is elated: suddenly his house is so spacious and clean and quiet.

I have thought of this story repeatedly throughout my work promoting human rights for Palestinians. How much of our work is simply removing the goat? Are we merely making an unbearable situation just-about bearable, while the underlying, untenable situation – prolonged military occupation – continues?

For families like Ala's, removing a checkpoint can mean the difference between life and death. We don't have the luxury of being cynical about this kind of achievement. I insist on celebrating the small victories, gaining strength and learning from them. At the same time, I hold fast to the vision of full rights for all, and continue to ask hard questions about the broader context of our work.

/ / /

The Drinking Fountain at the Checkpoint

The challenging human rights reality in the Occupied Palestinian Territory has been well documented. Human rights organisations have highlighted the full spectrum of rights violations in the West Bank, East Jerusalem and the Gaza Strip. Excessive force, violence, abuse, arbitrary detentions, and other restrictions are part and parcel of the Israeli occupation, now more than half a century old. Israel's military control is compounded by several structural phenomena that create systemic rights violations. These include the following factors, which strengthen and reinforce each other:

> The extensive settlement of the West Bank with Israeli civilians. Over half a million Israelis now live in the West Bank, including two hundred thousand in East Jerusalem. Israel exploits the natural resources in the West Bank for Israeli benefit, first and foremost land for the settlements, but also water, tourism sites, and quarries;
> The dual and highly discriminatory legal system in the West Bank in which Palestinians are subject to martial law and tried for offences in military courts, whereas settlers just down the road (and in some cases even right next door) and theoretically subject to the same law, enjoy the rights and privileges of Israeli citizens in all aspects of their life;
> The fragmentation of the Palestinian territories, both as a result of the Oslo Accords and subsequent Israeli policies. Israel has completely isolated the Gaza Strip and severed East Jerusalem from the rest of the West Bank. The West Bank is divided into three types of jurisdiction (Areas A, B & C). Since the 2007 political division between the West Bank and

the Gaza Strip, Palestinians are now subject to three different governing authorities – Israel, the Palestinian Authority and Hamas – all of which have a record of human rights violations;
> Large scale Israeli military operations in the Gaza Strip in response to Palestinian rocket-fire into Israel have wreaked enormous destruction of property and infrastructure, and claimed a high price in civilian lives.

The occupation is the primary source of Israeli violations against Palestinians' human rights; indeed such violations are an inevitable part of a prolonged occupation. This does not mean that an end to the occupation guarantees Palestinians will be able to enjoy basic rights – both the Palestinian Authority and the Hamas government in Gaza have poor human rights records vis-á-vis their own citizens and Israeli civilians. But certainly, the opposite is also true: so long as the occupation continues so will human rights violations. Consequently, Israeli human rights organisations will have work to do to address those violations.

This work is difficult, unpopular and full of dilemmas. At the start of October 2000, the Israeli military imposed extremely harsh restrictions on the movement of Palestinians inside the West Bank. A closure was imposed on each city, with checkpoints controlling all movement in and out. The conditions at these checkpoints were horrible, with people waiting hours in the hot sun with no amenities in order to move from one town to the next. Forty-eight Palestinians died after being delayed access to medical care, including seven newborn infants whose mothers gave birth to them at the checkpoints.

The Drinking Fountain at the Checkpoint

For several years, this was a central advocacy issue for the human rights community: the harsh conditions at the checkpoints, the blanket prohibition on young men from leaving the city of Nablus, the lack of regulations for free movement of people with medical emergencies. As I wrote above, today most of the internal West Bank checkpoints have been lifted. Those that remain include shaded waiting areas and drinking fountains.

The 'drinking fountain at the checkpoint' became the metaphor invoked by human rights activists to call into question the work we were doing. Rather than removing the illegal checkpoints, the argument goes, we have merely succeeded in ameliorating the suffering there, and in doing so, perhaps entrenched the checkpoints further. Some activists argue that the human rights community constitutes another organ of the occupation, pointing to the fact that, in spite of, or perhaps partly because of, our work, the occupation is even stronger than ever. We essentially make the intolerable tolerable and therefore permanent.

I have heard critics phrase this even more harshly: 'If there were no human rights organisations, no humanitarian aid organisations, the occupation would collapse within a year.' This may or may not be true; however, to my mind it is an irrelevant concern for a human rights activist. The idea that people can be used as instruments – that individuals' suffering is instrumental in advancing a political change, no matter how desirable – runs counter to the very essence of human rights.

So, we cannot neglect the individual case and the concrete manifestations of occupation that cause such suffering. Part of the work of the human rights community must be to assist victims of human rights violations regardless of the broader context. So, we must use the tools available to us to try to protect people from violence, to work to obtain permits for people who need them, and even (to take the example to the extreme) to ensure there is a drinking fountain at the checkpoint – even if that checkpoint should not have been erected in the first place.

And what of that broader context? We cannot just ignore it, yet factoring it into our work poses additional dilemmas. Take the Israeli High Court for example. This court enjoys immense prestige, both domestically and internationally. Its advocates take particular pride in the fact that the court is accessible to every Palestinian from the occupied territories and that it issues judgements, sometimes in real time, on issues regarding the conduct of military activities.

While the accessibility of the court is indeed a unique phenomenon, the rulings of the high court engender much criticism from the human rights community. On matters of principle and petitions challenging policy, the court rarely sides with human rights organisations against government or military policy. The high court has consistently either refused to rule or has ruled in favour of virtually all elements fundamental to the occupation itself: settlements, Palestinian home demolitions, and exploitation of resources for Israeli benefit. Both in its role as some form of pressure valve in individual cases and in the mantle of legality it affords to immoral and unjust policies, the court can serve as one of the mechanisms that enable the occupation to continue in its current form. Indeed, there have been voices calling for a boycott of the high court, in order to avoid giving the occupation a veneer of legality.

The Drinking Fountain at the Checkpoint

Nonetheless, the court has played a central role in virtually every human rights achievement. The advocacy against torture is a clear example. In the 1980s and 1990s, the human rights community documented a practice of systematic torture of Palestinians in interrogations by the Israeli Security Agency ('ISA' also known by its Hebrew initials the Shabak). After taking hundreds of testimonies and writing detailed reports, we built both the factual case (what is taking place is torture) and the legal case (torture is immoral and illegal). Initially, the Israeli government denied that Palestinians were being physically abused in interrogations. Human rights groups brought testimonies of Palestinians subjected to various forms of abuse in interrogation. The government subsequently denied the scale of the violations. Again, the human rights community was central in demonstrating that various forms of abuse were standard practice in the interrogation of hundreds of people. The government then argued that even if such practices were being used, they did not constitute torture, or that 'the defence of necessity' entitled interrogators to take 'exceptional measures' in response to so-called 'ticking bomb' situations.

One of the leaders of Amnesty International during this period remarked to me that torture was the one abuse that virtually every country committed, but that every country denied. Israel was the exception to the rule because it attempted to provide legal justifications for torture. The campaign by human rights organisations to stop torture took place during periods of intense violence – the first intifada and then the suicide bombings of the late-1990s. The ISA and its defenders claimed that torture was necessary to keep us safe. In the climate of very real fear for personal safety, the 'ticking bomb' thought experiment served as a powerful rationale for torture. What if a person who knows the specific details of a deadly and imminent attack against civilians is captured – would it be okay to extract this information using torture? For human rights organisations the answer is no: the state cannot turn human beings into instruments of its will. For many Israelis, feeling nervous every time their loved ones rode a bus or entered a shopping mall, the answer was yes: the state should do whatever it needs to do in order to keep us safe.

The 'ticking bomb' was a purely hypothetical situation – there were no known cases where Israeli forces held a person in custody and knew that information he possessed was necessary to prevent an imminent attack. On the rhetorical level, however, it constituted a very real challenge to building opposition to torture, both on the part of the public and even in the high court.

The principled petition against torture was filed in 1994 yet the court avoided issuing a ruling. Over the next five years organisations and attorneys filed one hundred and fifty individual petitions on behalf of Palestinians under interrogation. While the court never issued a ruling stopping torture in these individual cases, it appears this strategy, together with the concerns voiced by the international legal community, wore down the court. In 1999, the court finally ruled that the Israel Security Agency had no authority to use physical force in interrogations of Palestinians.

But was this ruling effective? Leah Tsemel was one of the lawyers heavily involved in the advocacy against torture. She visited detention centres seeking to meet Palestinians who were being interrogated and filed high court petitions, challenging the legality of torture in principle and trying to stop torture in real time. I met Leah some time after the high court handed down its historic ruling. She told of meeting her Palestinian clients right after the ruling. Men, who only the day before were subjected to various forms of abuse, told her how, almost miraculously, the torture had ceased. While there were still cases of abuse, this ruling resulted in an immediate halt to what had been the systematic torture of hundreds of Palestinians every year in ISA interrogations.

The high court was a crucial component of the successful campaign against systematic torture. It has played an important role in many other human rights struggles as well, both in realising individuals' rights and in forcing changes to policy.

And therein lies the dilemma. Many argue persuasively that the high court serves as a 'fig leaf' of the occupation. An organisation advancing a strategy to end the occupation would be wise to refrain from engagement with the court. Yet a human rights organisation fails in its mission if it prefers this macro-agenda at the expense of the individual human beings who are suffering and who the court can assist. Following analysis and debate regarding the high court, many organisations have adopted a compromise approach of only petitioning the high court on behalf of individuals. They will not ask the high court to rule on the principled issues involved in these cases.

So human rights organisations must be aware of the broader context in which we work, and remain true to the underlying principle of human rights – the unique value of every human being – while also acknowledging the complexities of doing this work in a context of occupation.

And do we have a role in tackling the occupation itself? I contend that ending the occupation is a political project and one with which human rights activists should be wary of getting involved. Human rights organisations do not have the tools to engage in the diplomatic process necessary to end the occupation. The modalities of negotiations and agreements necessary to achieve such an end are outside the scope of human rights organisations. Neither are we well-positioned to build the domestic constituency for peace and the compromises a peace agreement will require.

I have struggled with this question: how can we remain true to our human rights DNA while meaningfully addressing the root causes of human rights violations? Certainly, we have an important voice in shaping the public conversation. Much of our work is in the realm of 'naming and shaming': issuing reports, generating public awareness, ensuring media coverage and social media debates. In this public conversation we must not only point out individual cases but highlight the bigger picture: to show the moral and legal bankruptcy of prolonged military control over a civilian population and the exploitation inherent in the settlement enterprise.

/ / /

In the face of such debates, and the allegation that our work may be doing more harm than good, it is easy to despair. Indeed, our tendency as a human rights community is to focus on the despair, rather than our successes. Human rights activists are inherently critical. Our job is to identify what is wrong and try

The Drinking Fountain at the Checkpoint

to fix it. So, we always see what is wrong. There is no doubt that quite a bit is wrong when it comes to the state of human rights in Israel-Palestine. Yet even when we make gains our tendency is to highlight what is left to do rather than take pride in the achievement.

Our advocacy against punitive home demolitions is one of those cases where many will point to the half-empty glass. I insist on showing that the glass is in fact half-full. In my mind, of all Israeli policies that raise human rights concerns, punitive house demolitions are the clearest example of a collective punishment. The demolitions explicitly target innocent people: families whose only 'crime' is that they are related to Palestinians suspected of attacks against Israeli civilians and soldiers. The official objective of the house demolition policy is deterrence, based on the assumption that demolishing homes of the relatives of Palestinians who perpetrated, or are suspected of involvement in, these attacks would deter others from carrying out such attacks.

The scope of punitive home demolitions has risen and fallen over the past four decades but reached a peak during the second intifada. From October 2001 through 2004, the Israeli military demolished six hundred and sixty-four Palestinian homes as a punitive measure. In November 2004, the Israeli military established a committee, chaired by Major General Ehud Shani, to re-evaluate the policy of punitive house demolitions. In February 2005, then Minister of Defence, Shaul Mofaz, adopted the Shani Committee's recommendations to halt punitive house demolitions.

For the next decade, the Israeli security establishment did not demolish houses in the West Bank in response to attacks. During this period demolitions continued for other reasons: punitive house demolitions is only one of the legal frameworks under which the Israeli military demolishes Palestinian homes. In the decade following the decision to halt punitive demolitions, Israel carried out over one thousand three hundred 'administrative demolitions' in the West Bank and East Jerusalem – demolition of homes erected without building permits, which are extremely difficult for Palestinians to obtain. In addition, in Gaza the Israeli military destroyed thousands of homes in the course of military operations, in many cases far in excess of what international law would allow in such circumstances.

These other forms of demolition did not increase during the decade in which punitive demolitions halted. Without doubt, hundreds of families were spared the demolition of their home as a result of the policy change.

And what lead to the policy change? Certainly the human rights community constituted a driving force in causing the military to re-examine this policy. As early as 1989, Israel's High Court of Justice accepted the petition of the Association for Civil Rights in Israel (ACRI) and ruled that property owners had the right to appeal such demolitions. While these appeals rarely, if ever, stopped a demolition, it did cause a delay. The fact that demolitions could no longer be carried out immediately may have led to a subsequent decline in the use of punitive demolitions. At the height of the demolitions, during the second intifada, many organisations conducted advocacy campaigns against these demolitions, both inside Israel and around the world. HaMoked filed sixty-seven petitions to the high court against punitive home demolitions between 2002 and 2004.

The Drinking Fountain at the Checkpoint

An unusual hearing took place at the High Court of Justice in December 2004. HaMoked had petitioned against the demolition of the home of Mahmoud Ali Nasser, whose son was charged with recruiting the suicide bomber that killed seven people and wounded many others in the Hillel Cafe in Jerusalem on 9 August 2003. Attorney Andre Rosenthal, who was representing HaMoked, recalled that at the hearing, Justices Hayut, Cheshin and President Barak (the latter two approaching their retirement from the court) posed hard questions to the state's representative regarding the legality and morality of punitive home demolitions. 'Did the father even know what his son was about to do?' one justice asked. 'Why should his sister also be made to suffer? Isn't this a collective punishment?' another said. 'This was unprecedented. It's supposed to be my job to ask these questions,' Andre joked while retelling this story. 'I just sat back and let the justices barrage him with questions, while he turned pale.'

The hearing concluded with the court declaring a ninety-day postponement 'in order for the sides to consider a proposal in which only one room on the second floor would be demolished or sealed'. It was in this ninety-day period that the Shani Committee recommended the halt to all punitive home demolitions.

The proceedings and conclusions of the Shani Committee have remained classified. However, in the course of legal challenges to the renewal of home demolitions, HaMoked received a PowerPoint presentation prepared by the military regarding the committee's work. It is a fascinating document, a rare glimpse into the thought process within the military on these issues. Laid out in bullet points, the presentation gives both the military's rationale for the demolitions, and also raises questions about its effectiveness and legality:

> 'A tool in counter-terrorism – house demolitions demonstratively lead to investing terror's money in compensating families, even harming other terror activity;
> Deterrence – House demolitions have been proven to constitute an additional factor in deterring terrorists;
> Everything depends on the context – house demolitions as strengthening the national identity of the Palestinian collective;
> 'Liberalism' – in a state that committed itself to values of liberalism and democracy, house demolitions are viewed as collective punishment that do not accord with the principle of human dignity and property rights.'

The presentation goes on to suggest that house demolitions achieve the opposite effect from that intended:

> 'The activity harms individuals – but in large numbers;
> The activity damages personal property – but in large numbers;
> Fanning hatred;
> Strengthening collective public identity;
> Encouraging terrorism.'

The presentation concludes that: 'The price of the demolition in its broadest sense has intensified compared to its usefulness.'[1] 'Demolition of homes, particularly in refugee camps, intensifies the refugee trauma from the past ... IDF operations create "an unbridgeable chasm" – what will "the day after" look like?! The deterrent value of demolitions has been eroded.'

Interestingly, the presentation addresses all forms of home demolitions, including administrative demolition of homes built without permits. The presentation (rightly) points out that in the eyes of the Palestinians, all forms of demolition advance Israel's agenda. The military presentation concludes by recommending the reduction or halting of *all* forms of home demolition.

We cannot be certain as to the extent that the presentation accurately reflects the Shani Committee's treatment of the issue, but the presentation includes three different sets of arguments for halting punitive home demolitions:

> international criticism;
> legality and morality – after decades in which the military demolished homes with the approval of the High Court of Justice, it would be impossible for this committee to categorically determine that punitive demolitions are illegal. They therefore phrase these claims obliquely: 'the action is legal but is liable to not stand the test of legitimacy'; 'house demolitions are viewed as collective punishment'. However, it is clear that legal and moral concerns played a crucial role in the committee's deliberations;
> effectiveness – the official justification is that the policy is not effective as a deterrent.

The moratorium on punitive home demolitions is to be celebrated – and it is also to be learned from. The military's own rationale for halting these demolitions explicitly shows they are sensitive to international criticism and also to notions of both legality and morality. The presentation also clearly shows there is no zero-sum game between Israelis' security and Palestinian human rights – the military came to the conclusion that punitive home demolitions harm both. Each of these conclusions are relevant for other human rights struggles: we must continue advocacy both on the domestic and the international level; we must continue to highlight the moral and legal implications of these policies and we must show that many policies justified in the name of Israeli security are in fact counter-productive.

Sadly, the story of home demolitions does not end with the moratorium. In the summer of 2014, following the abduction and murder of three Israeli teenagers in the West Bank, the security establishment announced the resumption of punitive house demolitions. In the two years since this decision, the Israeli military demolished thirty-three families' homes as a punishment for the alleged acts of one of their family members.

This is a setback for human rights, but it does not erase the gains we have made. The battle against home demolitions has resumed, but from a stronger position than before. The military has acknowledged that home demolitions are not effective and probably counter-productive as a deterrent to violence. This acknowledgement is a powerful tool, and in high court cases over the past year we see that the judges are troubled as never before.

In spite of all of the obstacles and all of the setbacks, the human rights community has succeeded in making an impact during two decades of human rights advocacy. We have successfully advocated for hundreds of thousands of people.

The Drinking Fountain at the Checkpoint

We have managed to change policy for the better and prevent further deterioration.

This is not merely about getting a drinking fountain at the checkpoint. It is about saving lives, saving homes, stopping violence and allowing people to live in dignity. Our achievements are invariably partial and imperfect. This is the Sisyphean nature of human rights work. We are only one part of a larger system – the political project of ending the occupation must be left to others, while our public advocacy can keep the occupation on the agenda. So, there is much work left to be done, but this does not deter me. 'It is not on you to complete the task,' the Talmud teaches us. 'But neither are you free to desist from it.'

Note
1. PowerPoint presentation provided to author by HaMoked. Previous slides indicate that the 'price of the demolition' refers both to the international condemnation, as well as the resentment created among Palestinians.

Fragmented Hope

Nasser Alissa (Attalah)

A RIGHT IS NEVER LOST, AS LONG AS SOMEONE
STRIVES TO CLAIM IT – *Arabic saying*

Today, my neighbour, Ahmad, was released from an Israeli prison. Many people came to welcome him home, including my son Zaid, who will soon turn five. Upon his return, Zaid was carrying a flag of one of the Palestinian political parties. He told me that his friend Nour's dad was free from jail. Before I asked, he told me that Nour's father threw stones at the Israeli army because they took our village, Zakaria.

I discovered that Zaid had bigger dreams. He wanted to return to Zakaria. He asked me if the internet would be fast there, and if there were a lot of toys. He added that he wouldn't throw stones at the Israeli soldiers, but will 'hit them with a cream that burns their faces'. He asked me if I would go back there with him and if we had a house there, just like his grandmother and grandfather. There were dozens of difficult and frightening questions that began to preoccupy his young mind.

/ / /

In the camp, knowledge is passed on through generations, information shared through stories of our ancestors. The dream of return has not faded, but hopes have changed with age. My mother and father used to dream of returning to their home; now they dream of being buried in the shade under a fig tree or olive tree in their village.

The camp reinforces these values: that what is happening is temporary. These utopian and revolutionary tendencies are mutually justified, meaning that what some people can't imagine happening, I believe we can achieve. Nostalgia for a place, a right we have, nurtures hope in every person in the camp and personalises it despite the long series of events, massacres and displacement.

///

My consciousness was shaped in the camp through a series of experiences and stories that I lived through, in addition to the stories of my mother, father and grandparents about Zakaria and the Nakba. I still have some memories from when I was about five or a little older, memories that have turned into stories for the collective consciousness of life in the camps. When I think of these events, some of which sound accidental or even absurd, I cannot but think that they were arranged in order to change consciousness towards the absence of rights and replace them with pity; that UNWRA provides us with aid under Israeli occupation; that we should improve the status quo, rather than change it.

///

Fragmented Hope

The 1970s and 1980s witnessed a surge in assistance from the United Nations Relief and Works Agency for Palestine Refugees in the Near East (UNRWA) in the West Bank and Gaza's camps.

I remember how naïve I was when electricity reached the camp in 1976. We thought that television would come along with it, but it did not.

/ / /

Among the supplies distributed by the agency, such as milk, oil and rice, were second-hand European and American clothes. I remember queuing with my mother for hours outside UNRWA's headquarters for the clothes – we used to call them *bukja* (packages) – to be distributed. It was like a lottery: lucky ones might find a variety of clothes; the unlucky ones would get hundreds of neckties or hats.

Mothers would then organise exchange sessions and would rearrange everything according to size, gender, items of clothing. Many of the clothes wouldn't fit any of us, in particular those that came from America as they were all extra-large sizes.

But each time this happened, the day after bukjas had been distributed, people would be walking around the camp wearing hats, jackets, Charleston pants, all American and European styles.

One of my friends used to say that it wasn't supposed to be funny. That it was about turning the camp into a society that depended on aid. Our situation had become a humanitarian cause; we were no longer considered refugees who had been displaced from their homes and had a right to go home.

DEFENDING HOPE

///

Like other young people in the camp, I was influenced by the great revolutionary left-wing movements that idolised Che Guevara and Russian novelists of the Second World War. Although perhaps at times misguided, this was our intellectual food that gave us energy to face the occupier.

As children, confronting the occupying soldiers made complete sense. We did not need any motivation; we witnessed daily attacks by settlers driving by our camps, the same settlers who had taken our land to build their own homes. We didn't know where their hatred came from, but it generated a lot of anger inside us. We were being punished with occupation and punished by the settlers' attacks on us.

///

I was fifteen when I started smoking. I was fifteen the first time I was arrested. Around fifty soldiers surrounded our house and started banging on the door. My father opened, ten entered, they asked, 'Where is Nasser?' My mother replied, 'He is just a kid, what do you want with him?' A soldier said, 'We will ask him some questions and then release him'.

I opened my eyes. A soldier was pointing his gun to my head. It was 1 a.m. My mother gave me $2 and told me: 'Don't worry, you will be back soon, you are my hero.' She was strong in a way that made me afraid.

After a two-hour drive, we arrived at the interrogation centre. The party began.

Fragmented Hope

Handcuffs and blindfold. Made to stand up the whole time. First question: 'Who are your friends?' 'I don't have any.' 'What are the names of your teachers?' 'I cannot remember.' 'You throw stones at settlers?' (Yes, I did.) I told them, 'No, I didn't.'

The fist slap in the face was really bad; after that I lost all feeling. After beating every part of my body, my interrogator got tired and asked for help. Others came and began a new session of torture. I was thinking of my mother: I am her hero.

Eighteen days. No sleep. Soaking in cold water. Daily torture sessions. Some hours of relaxation, but I couldn't sleep. I was thinking of two things: my friends will be going on a trip and I missed it; and it's snowing. I love snow.

I was told that if I smoked, I could sleep. It was true. I'm still smoking today.

My advice: don't arrest children – they might become smokers.

///

I want to be liberated. That's the power I want. I don't seek revenge from those who tortured me, but I want them held accountable. I want them to say sorry. Then I will send them home to their families.

If you recognise the pain of others and that you are the reason for this pain, then we can move a step forward.

///

DEFENDING **HOPE**

I was arrested and detained about twelve times during my childhood. Each detention would last between eighteen and forty days. We were all subjected to various kinds of physical torture: beatings, being tied by our hands and hung for days, deprived of sleep for days, soaked in cold water during winter. Most children were sexually abused. I cannot say that they were raped by someone, but I did see children forced to sit naked on glass bottles. (Do not ask me if this happened to me) Many children were forced to masturbate while a group of interrogators would watch and laugh.

But it served no purpose, they were unable to get us to confess, even though what confession meant was admitting to raising a Palestinian flag, writing slogans against occupation on walls or throwing a stone at soldiers invading the camps. What our interrogators didn't realise was that children had enormous energy and tolerance in the face of injustice.

/ / /

In truth, we are narcissists. We believe that our sun and moon are the most beautiful of all. We believe that we are the best and most beautiful people, that we love this life, that our mothers are the beautiful saints, and that our bread, our olives, our thyme and our wheat have irresistible magic.

/ / /

I spent the beginning of 1986 in solitary confinement. At 10 p.m., it was lights out and silence. But on new year's eve, we decided

Fragmented Hope

to celebrate. Around 11 p.m., we began singing loudly. A soldier came: *shhhhhhhh!* But we continued singing and used a table as drums. All other sections were watching, some were laughing. Lots of soldiers arrived. This is what happens when you lock up children, someone shouted.

/ / /

Despite the high price we paid, I wanted this intifada to last longer. The solidarity among the people was beautiful: neighbours exchanging bread and food, everyone opening their houses and providing a safe place for the wanted activists.

Women broke barriers during the first intifada and changed the traditional role of Arab and Palestinian women. All sectors of society were participating in demonstrations, but women were at the heart of the struggle; they threw rocks, distributed leaflets and confronted soldiers with their bodies. They created cooperatives to overcome the scarcity of resources and reduce the dependence on Israeli products.

I remember all the mothers whose homes I grew up in. They would prepare food for my friends and I. They would confront soldiers when they came to give us time to escape. One of these women was my aunt; I still have pain in my heart because I was unable to say goodbye to her. She was beaten to death in her house by soldiers. I was in the Negev prison and word only reached me a month later through a friend.

/ / /

DEFENDING **HOPE**

My detainee number was 3444. It was May 1988 and I arrived at Ktzi'ot detention centre. Hundreds of tents, sand everywhere, faces covered in dust watching me. We had to run as there were soldiers on both sides hitting us with batons. I tried to protect an old man beside me who couldn't run fast enough. Later that night I found my brother with a broken hand. I gave him some chewing gum that I had managed to hide. He asked me about his newborn son; I told him we named him Nidal.

///

In 1988, Yitzhak Rabin, the Israeli Defence Minister, visited the Negev prison. I remember something he said to our section: 'As long as there is an intifada, there will be a first, and second, and third Negev.' I believe that as long as the occupation exists; there will be a third, fourth, fifth and sixth intifada.

///

My friend Shuaib decided to wash his underwear, he never found it again. After that we were always guarding our underwear. Most of us spent six months with one pair. Many had none. Till this day, I still have nightmares that someone is trying to steal my underwear and I'm running, running, running. I bought dozens of pairs of underwear.

///

Fragmented Hope

My hope is that all these horrible things will not happen to our children. But you know what, I can't write about hope …*wallah* I can't. Sorry.

/ / /

Winter nights were terrible, getting colder and colder until it reached my bones. I can still remember the smell of the toasted bread and avocado that the guards would eat when I was so hungry. Saturdays were the worst, it was party night: interrogation would last all night, there would be two interrogators. I still have dreams about it.

/ / /

Civil disobedience was another marker of the intifada. The town of Beit Sahour became a model for civil disobedience. The town decided to boycott Israeli products, refused to pay taxes to the occupation and formed popular committees to create economic and educational alternatives. A film was recently made, *The Wanted 18*, which tells the story of Beit Sahour and the eighteen cows the town had purchased from a kibbutz to provide milk for the whole village. According to Israel, the cows were a threat to national security and had to be confiscated.

/ / /

The hardest thing about prison wasn't the beatings, the deprivation of food, the cold, the lack of water, it's the state of

DEFENDING **HOPE**

disconnection from the outside world and the denial of family visits. I was worried about my family and friends, afraid I'd lose one of them during daily invasions and confrontations with soldiers in the camp. And of course, I did lose friends.

///

Even in the toughest conditions, we kept hope and we developed little coping mechanisms. For example, we used to hide the Hebrew newspapers we found in the garbage when we moved them into containers. We brought them into our sections and translated the political articles. The guards didn't know that we could read Hebrew of course. We also had to hide magazines we found from the Palestinian prison supervisors, especially those containing pictures of girls as they were cutting out anything they thought inappropriate.

///

We planted melons and watermelons. It was our refuge, a place where we gathered, watered them and watched them growing. One day soldiers came and removed them; they told us it was against prison rules. I remember one of the detainees cried, as if he had lost a close friend.

///

My mother, for years and years, kept telling me to 'keep some hope son'. I want to be released from my fear first. The truth is, every time I travel and when I get stopped at the border, my heart begins beating fast. 'Did I write anything? Has someone told them anything about me?' I'm afraid to speak or write or share my opinion. I don't want to go back to prison. I want this power that destroyed my soul to disappear.

///

Detainees who were released would carry letters from other detainees to their loved ones. Those released were thoroughly searched before they left, so letters would be written in tiny fonts on tiny pieces of paper that we would insert into capsules. Those released would then either swallow them or stick them up their backsides.

I did not write to my girlfriend about the abuse and the beatings, I wrote about the sunset in the desert, comparing it to the sunset on our land in the mountains. I wrote about the first cat that came to the place and how dozens of us would gather by the fence to observe it. I wrote to her about the birds that came to us looking for water.

///

In 1992, I went back to university after a three-year closure. I had started studying social work and psychology in 1987 before being arrested. What I really wanted to study was philosophy; I had been very influenced by Plato, Hegel, Feuerbach, Engels, Marx and Frantz Fanon, and believed that students were the key to change, but it was not available in local universities.

DEFENDING HOPE

///

In 1995, I began working with Defence for Children International – Palestine (DCI) in Hebron. I worked with children who had been injured or who had witnessed the Ibrahimi Mosque massacre. I visited them in their homes and schools, I talked to them about what they witnessed. I felt my work was a failure, I felt incapable of helping them. Some may say that listening to them is in itself an achievement, but that is never true, especially in the case of these children.

Despite feeling helpless, I continued. The mothers were happy that at least someone was listening to them and trying to bring them joy. The other reason was that our presence bothered the soldiers. They even broke into our offices at night, destroyed the furniture and later arrested my colleague.

///

What does it mean to be a human rights defender in this country? You will never know how many children you helped. You will never know how many will complete their education, how many will become teachers, writers, poets or politicians. But I think it's not important.

///

In September 2000, the second intifada erupted, sparked by Ariel Sharon's visit to the Al-Aqsa Mosque.

Fragmented Hope

Children were greatly affected by this intifada, and not just because of school closures, curfews, lack of food and healthcare, but also because of the frequent killings, further repression and daily invasions in the camp that were part of a deliberate tactic of spreading fear and panic for the entire population.

So, we decided to form a large team of volunteers throughout the West Bank and Gaza. Hundreds joined. Most of them were social work and psychology students. We trained them so that they could visit homes and families and talk about how to deal with children, how to listen, what to do when there is shelling, and how to provide some security for children.

///

The truth is, it was a taboo to lose hope. As child rights activists, we turned into fighters, but not fighters with weapons; instead we worked like ambulance crews in order to reach out to many houses to bring emotional and psychological support.

///

The second intifada was the worst period for travelling. We were forbidden from going to the airport in Israel. The only choice was to travel to Jordan through Jericho, the lowest city in the world, two hundred and fifty-eight metres below sea level. The worst of all four hundred checkpoints.

'Will you let me enter?' I asked one of the soldiers. Hundreds of us were waiting in the heat, at least forty-five degrees. 'Okay,' said one soldier, 'here is the order: I will play a song, the first one to name it, he gets to pass.' I am good at music; well, I'm not bad if they're old songs. My God, I did recognise it. 'This is Fairouz,' I said. 'Raise your hand and wait,' said the soldier. 'Okay, Okay,' I raised my hand. It was the right answer. Checkpoint champion. I passed.

/ / /

As Palestinians, we believe that we will not win the battle with the occupation by one strike, but rather by points. I recently asked a youth who often participates in protests, 'Do you think that a stone can win over a bullet?' 'This is a long ongoing battle,' he said, 'the winner will not win by knockout, but on points.'

/ / /

At the end of 2008, my wife decided to study for a PhD in Mental Health at the University of Manchester. Before my departure, I contacted the Child Rights International Network (CRIN) and offered to volunteer for them while in the UK. This was the beginning of a new life for us.

CRIN's work in the MENA region consisted mainly at this stage of providing information in Arabic. But I had noticed that their translator had been deliberately omitting information about sexuality and LGBTQ issues, information that people in our region would qualify as shameful or 'culturally inappropriate,' and without CRIN's knowledge. I wanted to rectify this, even though I know very well that many people in my region, including NGOs would disagree with me. I strongly believe that the work we are doing, spreading information and ideas, is crucial and is an investment for the future. It will take time for people to come around and accept them, but they will.

Once we returned to Palestine, I was appointed as their Regional Director for the Middle East and North Africa (MENA).

///

I look at young people today who were children during the second intifada and consider what they grew up with: these young people are those leading today's popular resistance.

///

There were many questions about children's participation when the Arab Spring erupted. Children, like adults, participated in many protest movements in Tunisia, Yemen, Egypt, Libya, Syria and as well as Palestine. And it led to the death, injury and arrest of many of them.

In my opinion, the right of children to participate is a sacred one that must be protected rather than prevented. If children must be protected, it is necessary to work against those who oppress them rather than suppress their participation to challenge their oppressors.

It is no secret that Palestinian children stabbed or attempted to stab Israelis. Of course, they were wrong, there is no doubt. But we must understand what leads them to such acts. Some have said that they were incited by the media, but children who have grown up under occupation, who have seen their father or mother humiliated on a daily basis, do not need incitement.

///

We say that the wounds of the soul are more difficult to recover than the wounds of the body, especially for the most vulnerable groups, such as the children.

///

Girls are yet again leading change and challenging traditions in the camp. This time in the form of a girls' rap band, supported by the organisation Shoruq.[1] The members of the band are refugees and they write their own lyrics on the right to return, life in the camp, occupation, recruitment of children to fight. This has given us a great deal of energy and hope for change.

///

Our role must be to raise awareness about participation, how it applies to children in different contexts, and how they can participate. Protection versus their right to protest is a dilemma, of course, but in my opinion, it is not our right to set a model for what is forbidden or permitted.

Equally, I do not have answers to how to protect children under occupation; its practices may kill a child in his or her school or home, its military laws may allow their arrest because they joined a funeral march or posted something against occupation on Facebook.

Fragmented Hope

///

On a personal level, working at CRIN changed my thoughts a lot. It's not just about how we work, with children, for them, or both. It is more about opening up choices for children and what our responsibility as adults is first, and secondly, as child and human rights defenders. CRIN taught me that the role of human rights defenders should not be limited to defending the rights of those who are most vulnerable. It should be directed also towards working to build new lives for them and contribute to the development of models that help them to grow and develop.

///

A few years ago, a man in his early twenties was killed by Israeli soldiers in the camp. My daughters, who were almost thirteen and fourteen at the time, asked me if they could participate in the funeral procession. I realised at that moment that my daughters had grown up and that they would eventually be involved, like other girls and boys, in such marches. How could I deny them their right to participate in the funeral of someone they knew well? Do I have the right to prevent them? As a child rights activist, I was afraid.

///

Christmas is arriving soon. Bethlehem is beautiful despite pain and injury. Santa Claus is on the front line, near the wall. He decided to celebrate with the children nearby, brought them gifts and candy; lots of people gathering around him.

Then everyone started running, military jeeps chasing them, live and rubber bullets, tear gas everywhere. Ambulances arrive, take away some of the wounded, come back. A sound bomb explodes nearby.

Santa got fed up, threw off his mask, joined the group and started throwing stones.

///

In our country, we cry when we dance, or when we watch people dance. I don't know why; perhaps because life doesn't treat us well, or because the only good thing we have is dancing. Some people have been arrested for dancing. Maybe it's one of the things occupation cannot take away from us.

///

The work of Shoruq and the children and young people participating in singing, dancing, painting, they teach us about hope and about optimism, about their suffering and their dreams.

What frightens me is losing one of them during night invasions. Because we have. Hundreds of children will go out of their homes to confront soldiers and throw stones. They are desperate, it's their daily reality, but they love life like any other child.

///

Fragmented Hope

The town of Beit Jala, across the valley from Bethlehem, woke up this evening, full of power and beauty. This morning's sadness and suffocating smell have been replaced by lights and people. Nothing will stop Beit Jala from celebrating, not the wall, not the siege. They want the best Christmas tree in the area; it has to be the tallest and the brightest. This is celebration in front of barrels of guns.

/ / /

As human rights defenders in Palestine, what is also required is a long-term action to free ourselves from occupation and to create a protective environment free from violence that is sensitive to the needs and rights of children and the most vulnerable groups.

We must also realise that our confrontation is not only with the occupation, it is also with the radical groups that try to impose their extremist ideas and terrorise others. In my opinion, they are as dangerous to children as the occupation is.

/ / /

Looks like your painting[2] couldn't protect the twelve-year-old Palestinian boy Shadi Obeidallah from Ayda camp. He was killed by a sniper less than a hundred metres away from the wall where your painting is. Just an hour ago. Bullet to the heart.

/ / /

Our family has a small piece of land in the mountains where we grow cucumbers, we have some olive trees and almond trees.

DEFENDING **HOPE**

Israelis discovered that we love watching the sunset there. So, they came with bulldozers in the early morning. They were discussing whether to demolish the house or the road. But they are smart. The bulldozers began digging up the road, they left the house intact. They want to burn our hearts, control our life. They can give and they can take. But we are smart too and we have the will and the strength. We came before sunset, we fixed the road. They'll come back. We are ready for the next battle.

/ / /

As human rights activists, we must accept that we might not reap the results of our work, that we are working for the future. Our work goes beyond a package of activities or events. As we seek to build model systems, laws and programmes, we are also striving to change a worn out and retroactive system of laws and regulations defended by individuals, organisations or even governments.

/ / /

Someone painted a guardian angel on the wall. Some people were angry: they think it brings bad luck. Many people have been killed or injured there. Some people think it's a symbol that reflects the situation here. I'm not for or against it; in reality I don't care. All I know is that all of us here need at least three guardian angels: to protect us from a stray bullet, from a stray soldier, from a stray state. I read this on a child's Facebook page.

Fragmented Hope

///

Ironically, human rights defenders are also vulnerable to prosecution, arrest, and threats by the Palestinian Authority's security services. The expression of your opinion or criticism on social media might be a pretext for arrest.

President Mahmoud Abbas recently ratified the Cyber Crimes Law. The law has sparked the anger of journalists and jurists as an attack on freedom of opinion and expression, restricting, in particular, the publication of materials on social networking sites, as well as putting people under surveillance by the security services. All of these in clear contravention of international human right standards. Issa Amro, a well-known human rights defender in the Hebron area, was recently arrested because he criticised the Palestinian authorities on Facebook.[3]

It's no different in the Gaza Strip under Hamas rule. They have also arrested or threatened activists for their articles or views published in the media or on social media.

///

Well, you asked me about hope in a time that I feel helpless.

///

In July 2014, Israeli soldiers shot and killed forty-four-year-old child rights activist Hashem Abu Mariya while he was in Beit Ummar village, Hebron district at a demonstration in solidarity with Gaza. For more than eight years, my friend Hashem and I had been working to advocate for children's rights and children's awareness of their rights.

The soldiers knew him well and he was arrested more than once. According to eyewitnesses, Hashem was not involved in the demonstration, but was standing at a distance from it. Hashem left behind him three children and a wife.

Many of us who knew Hashem and had worked with him, including children, were shocked by his death. I felt that I would not be able to continue working. Even in my worst nightmares, I had not expected Hashem to leave so early.

I was affected by what the children wrote about him, hundreds of messages on Facebook. I still meet some of those whom Hashem worked with after the year 2000 and later enrolled in university or graduated. What comforts me is the great impact he has left on them. I think that's enough to keep us all going.

/ / /

I watched a TV documentary about a British lady who started an initiative to care for abused donkeys. The donkeys get medical care, they have a dentist, they get good food. I wish was a donkey.

/ / /

I believe that the message of every human rights defender lies in exposing every violation wherever and regardless of who is responsible for it. Many regimes have tried to buy the silence of human rights defenders, either by intimidation or enticement tactics. Some defenders went as far as justifying the oppression of regimes. The same applies to those human rights organisations that receive funding from parties and governments that violate human rights. He who eats the bread of the king will strike with his sword.

///

We all love life. We just want it with some taste of dignity and a small amount of freedom. We want to breathe, to drink and eat but from our farms, not other people's farms, and again with honour.

///

The problems we face might not end for a hundred years. As activists and defenders of children's rights and human rights, we must realise this. We must also develop our ways to recharge our batteries. Maybe we have to take that energy from those children, in some ways, we all need each other.

///

Today, I made some birthday wishes for my son …

That he will listen to music, not news, when he is six. That he will go to a warm school when he is seven. That he will join a dancing group when he is eight. That he will stay in a fancy hotel in London when he is nine. That he will swim in the Mediterranean when he is ten. That he is free to do whatever

DEFENDING HOPE

he wants when he's eleven. That he will not throw stones when he is twelve. That he will not to be arrested when he is thirteen. That he will have a girlfriend when he is fourteen. That he will not smoke when he is fifteen. That we will have our airport and travel freely when he is sixteen. That we can drive without stopping at checkpoints when he is seventeen. That would mean we will have our own state when he is eighteen.

/ / /

Notes

1. Shoruq was established in 2013 in the Dheisheh refugee camp, with the support of CRIN and other organisations. Shoruq works with the most vulnerable children in the society, children who are in conflict with Palestinian laws, through a legal clinic that represents children. It also provides legal counselling and psychological support for them and their families. It also provides technical and media training programmes as well as an international advocacy programme for refugees.
2. A reference to a mural painted in 2015 in Bethlehem, Palestine by Miriam Sugranyes and CRIN colleagues. www.instagram.com/p/Bcjx5degB2h/?taken-by=miriamsugranyes/.
3. Peter Beaumont, 'Palestinian Authorities Arrest Activist Issa Amro in Growing Free Speech Crackdown', *The Guardian*, 5 September 2017. www.theguardian.com/world/2017/sep/05/palestinian-authorities-arrest-activist-issa-amro-in-growing-free-speech-crackdown/.

The Little Acts that Tip the Scales

Arik Ascherman

The philosopher of the Holocaust Emile Fackenheim tells a story of trying to order a telephone line in Israel. Back in the days when few people had them, getting a phone could take years. Speaking to the phone company, he said, 'So, there is no hope of getting a phone more quickly?' The clerk, not realising he was speaking to a world class philosopher (who taught that there is now a six hundred and fourteenth commandment, when traditional Judaism says there are six hundred and thirteen), did not want to give Hitler a posthumous victory by renouncing hope or faith, so he launched into a long lecture about how it is forbidden to give up hope.

'So, I might get the line sooner?' Fackenheim asked.

'No chance,' came the reply, 'but don't give up hope.'

Emile Fackenheim could have dedicated this story to the cause of building peace between Palestinians and Israelis.

When I was young I had little to do with the conflict between Palestinians and Israel. I grew up in Erie, Pennsylvania, with a population of one hundred and thirty-eight thousand. Mine was a family hugely committed to Israel and as a young boy I dreamed I would go to Israel. From the age of seven I also wanted to be a rabbi. We lived in a Jewish community about one hundred years old. But, as I became more conscious of the world around me, it was South Africa, not Israel, which first drew my attention as an activist. For a long time, I believed that I would make my contribution to *tikkun olam* (what many Christians call 'co-creationism' – being God's partners in the ongoing work of creation) in Africa. I was involved in the Anti-Apartheid Movement and many other political and social justice movements throughout my days in university, spending more time organising protests or trying to educate other students than studying. But for me the first priority remained becoming a rabbi. I was also very involved in Jewish activities on campus, sometimes wishing there were more people making the connection I saw between them. There were many Jews in the Anti-Apartheid Movement who were not at all Jewishly identified. Few active in Jewish life seemed interested in applying the values that shouted to me from our Jewish texts.

At the first opportunity I applied to the Hebrew Union College for rabbinical school. The day I received a letter back was one of enormous excitement. I was too nervous to open the envelope. And rightly so; my dreams were dashed – I had been rejected.

The college told me that they could see how committed I was to Judaism but they believed I lacked experience in the world. I had spent too much time going from school to school and needed to get out and experience the world. As I had long believed that the responsibility for my partnership with God to improve the world lay in South Africa, now it seemed obvious that I would go to join the front lines of the movement there. The anti-apartheid activist Steve Biko had died a few years before as a result of a serious beating by the South African police. South African students and unions were organising boycotts of schools and factories, like Colgate, and the world was responding. I had been involved in an intense struggle with the university to divest

The Little Acts that Tip the Scales

its holdings from companies that were doing business in South Africa. (A year after I graduated the campaign was successful.) The issue was the hot social justice topic of our times. I thought I would live my life wherever I could make my greatest contribution to *tikkun olam*.

However, just as all this was happening, I heard about a programme in Israel called 'Interns for Peace', a community work programme bringing together Israeli Jews, Israeli Arabs and people like myself from abroad, to create better relations between Israeli Arabs and Israeli Jews. Many people don't realise that in addition to the Palestinians in the occupied territories captured by Israel in 1967, some 20 per cent of Israeli citizens are actually Christian and Muslim Palestinians with Israeli citizenship. I was really excited about this programme, but my blinkers were still on, and I was going to rabbinical school. When I was told I needed to do something in the world beforehand, I knew just what I wanted to do. Conveniently, this was what my rabbinical college wanted too.

My first shock upon arriving in Israel was that they had no bagels. What kind of a Jewish State could this be without bagels?! But I also experienced a more profound shock. Growing up in Pennsylvania, my parents, my teachers and my rabbis informed me that to be Jewish was to be committed to universal rights and social justice. But I found that these views were not shared by many Israelis. Things I never would have dreamed of questioning, that were so axiomatic to me, were marginalised in Israel. While Israel was broadly a democratic country, within its borders I encountered a problematic combination of extreme nationalism and particularism. I saw this first hand for the (almost) two years I lived in the Israeli Arab village of Tamra in the Galilee while trying to build coexistence programmes with the nearby Jewish community of Kiryat Ata. (Not to be confused with the settlement of Kiryat Arba in the occupied territories.)

Many times, long and painful discussions with Israeli Arabs about the various forms of discrimination they suffered would end with a comment that, 'We could live with all of that, if only Jewish Israelis would view us as Israelis as well.'

I had begun to call myself a Zionist at the university. I had come to realise that there were strands of Zionism which I found repugnant and racist, while strongly identifying with others. The common denominator was that Zionism was the liberation movement of the Jewish people. I still believe that being a Zionist is part of a commitment to the liberation of the Jewish people – but when that liberation comes at the cost of another people's freedom it is not representative of Jewish values.

The Jewish tradition teaches us to believe that, even when all is dark, we must maintain our faith that with God's guidance, the arc of history will ultimately bring us to a more just, healed and sanctified world. We each have our role to play in bringing that world about. Despair is an option we are not permitted. Judaism teaches that, while there has never been a human being that has not done wrong, our true selves are pure and good. The word for 'repentance' in Hebrew (*teshuvah*) shares the same root as the word for 'return'. At one level, *teshuvah* is about improving our behaviour as individuals. However, some of what we need to correct is at a societal level. By working for justice we are returning to our truest and highest selves.

The Little Acts that Tip the Scales

Of course, in the midst of such noble ideas the work is complex and sensitive. I had originally thought I was coming to lead protests, as I had against apartheid. My work in the Galilee was less focused on organising people in protest at the conditions of their lives and more on doing projects to serve Jews and Arabs and to bring them together to reach a common understanding.

And the gap in understanding between the two peoples was enormous. Israel's invasion of Lebanon occurred while I was there. I was forbidden by my organisation to get involved in anything deemed as political activity. People in my Arab village would say to me 'you're anti-war, why aren't you doing anything to stop this war?' This pressure from people I worked with every day, as well as my internal moral compass, meant I couldn't resist. I had to go. So, I would leave my village and secretly go to organise anti-war demonstrations in Haifa. When I came back to Tamra people asked why I wasn't doing anything to stop the war; it was very frustrating not to be able to tell people about my activities. But I would speak with people there who were afraid: they believed that Israel would extend its war to the Arabs living inside Israel. Many of them had lived memories, or passed on memories, of the 1948 destruction of Arab villages. When the massacres occurred in Sabra and Shatilla people I knew would say: 'That's it! We're next.' But, Israeli Jews couldn't believe that Israeli Arabs would actually think that. For their part, Israeli Jews were convinced that, now that Israel was at war, Israeli Arabs would act as a fifth column. Arabs did not believe that they could possibly be sharing their true feelings. 'How could they be afraid of us? Don't listen to the propaganda, Arik. They have the fourth most powerful army in the world.'

Similarly, when I would go to Kiryat Ata, the Jewish town, people would express surprise at the fact that I was working with Arabs. Jews felt they were surrounded by country after country where people hated them and wanted to see their annihilation. I knew from my work with Arabs that they, too, just wanted to live a normal life. But again people could not get past what they saw around them. I would often hear: 'Your own poor come first.'

As I continued my work I realised that no matter what I believed was right or wrong it was essential that I start to talk with people where they are at. This is how change happens. I could try to persuade people of my view and let them know that I thought they were exaggerating. However, unless I understood their view was real for them, I could never have the possibility of persuading them. I also needed to be a credible messenger. I realised that the gap in trust between peoples could not be bridged by simply speaking – I would have to live out my Jewish values in a very real way by standing directly in the path of injustice. This commitment needs to be wholehearted and I knew it would involve considerable risk to my own safety if I was truly to prove my commitment to Palestinians and Israelis.

We see this in the Midrash (rabbinic commentary on the Torah) when Jospeh descends into the darkness of Egypt, sold as a slave by his own son. Reuben was preoccupied with his inability to protect Joseph. Jacob was inconsolable after the death of his son while Judah was having an illicit relationship with his own daughter-in-law. Yet even in these bleak times God was sowing the seeds of redemption. Even though Judah had once thought nothing of selling his own brother into slavery he later offered to sacrifice himself to save Benjamin. The Book of Genesis is about

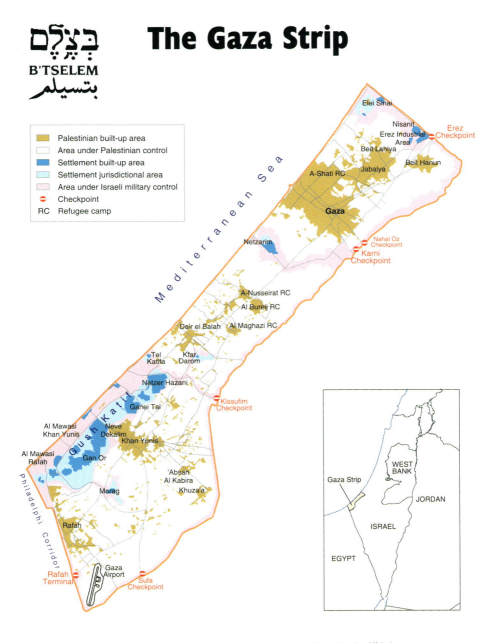

Fig. 1: Map of the Gaza Strip. (B'Tselem)

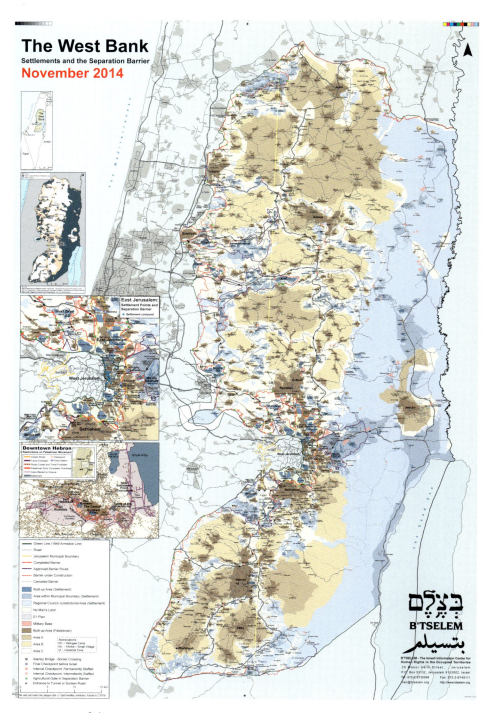

Fig. 2: Map of the West Bank showing the settlements and the wall. (B'Tselem)

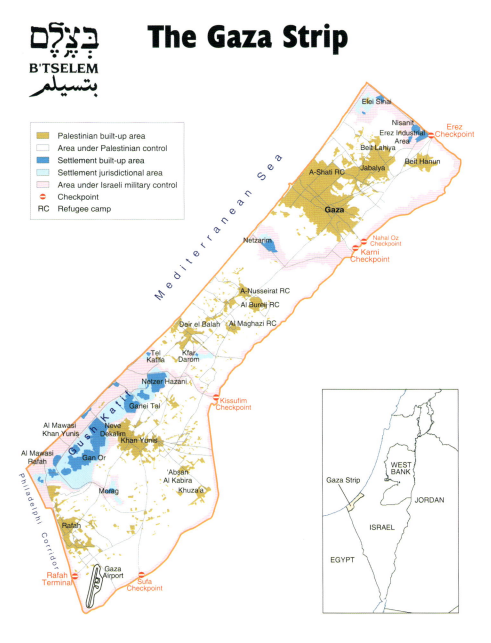

Fig. 1: Map of the Gaza Strip. (B'Tselem)

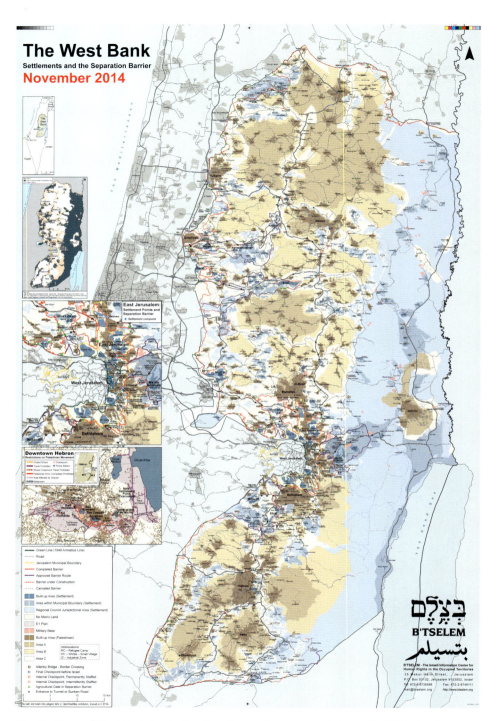

Fig. 2: Map of the West Bank showing the settlements and the wall. (B'Tselem)

Fig. 3: Sign forbidding Israeli citizens from entering Area A in the West Bank. Photo: Joanne O'Brien

Fig. 4: Gaza Port. Around thirty thousand Gazans depend on the fishing industry for their livelihood but fishermen face heavy movement restrictions imposed by the Israeli navy. Photo: Joanne O'Brien

Fig. 5: Woman in Gaza cooking over an open fire due to electricity shortages, 2016. Photo: Samar Abu Elouf

Fig. 6: Schoolgirls, Gaza City. In 2017, the charity Save the Children reported that one million Gazan children were living in dire conditions because of pollution and the lack of electricity and water. Photo: Joanne O'Brien

Fig. 7: Burns clinic at the Al Ahli Arab Hospital in Gaza City, 2016. Many children suffer domestic burns from the oil stoves that their mothers must use for cooking, because of the lack of electricity in Gaza due to the Israeli blockade.
Photo: Joanne O'Brien

Fig. 8: Paediatric outpatients clinic for malnourished and underweight children at the Al Ahli Arab Hospital in Gaza City, 2016. Many babies live on tea and bread, and 80 per cent of the population in Gaza requires food aid.
Photo: Joanne O'Brien

Fig. 10: Dr Hashem al-Azzeh, a well-known Hebron human rights defender stands in his barricaded home in the Old Town of Hebron, 2013. He died in October 2015 as a result of inhaling tear gas fired at a demonstration. Photo: Joanne O'Brien

Fig. 9: Armed settler on patrol in the Israeli controlled part of Hebron city.
Photo: Joanne O'Brien

The Little Acts that Tip the Scales

Judah – who changed – not about Joseph, the victim. We learn from this Midrash that people can and do change. This is the source of hope.

///

The other lesson that we learn from the Midrash is that some sacrifice is required to follow the path God has blessed. I can't pretend that my sacrifice is anything like that of a family whose home has been demolished for the tenth or eleventh time. Or that I can understand the pain of a mother who reaches out to forgive the Palestinian who killed her son while he remains in an Israeli prison. My sacrifice is nothing compared to them and in the face of building a society that represents the will of God my sacrifice is small. But if a bulldozer is about to demolish the home of a Palestinian family who have nowhere else to go my first responsibility is not to ask 'what flag is on the bulldozer?' or 'who paid for it?' My first responsibility is to do everything possible to stop the demolition. To me, standing in front of that bulldozer and placing my own safety at risk, irrespective of the possible cost, is the only choice.

In late 2015, thirty-three years after my arrival in Israel, I was helping Palestinian farmers harvest their olives. I had passed through many tests and realised many dreams: I had finally attended rabbinical college. My work with Palestinians allowed me to live out the Jewish values I held so dearly. For some years now I had been working with other Jewish and international activists to support Palestinians who are trying to access their farm-land despite threats from the settlers and closures by the

Israeli army. We try to have one foot on the ground, and the other in the corridors of power, including the Israeli court system. However, for me the significant part of the work is at the coalface of the conflict, in those dry hills surrounded by the olive trees themselves, building real human connections. So, one day in the hilly West Bank in the October sun, I knelt on a white tarpaulin spread under an ancient olive tree. A young Palestinian man was taking time off from his day job in the Palestinian Presidential Guards, a branch of the Palestinian Authority police force, to help his family harvest. He was beating the tree vigorously to knock the olives onto the tarpaulin. He was suspicious of my presence and seemed to be watching me closely. I think he had elected to work on my tree partially because he could not believe an Israeli rabbi would help his family and partially out of curiosity to learn more about me. Perhaps he wondered if I was a spy from the Israeli security services or, even worse, a settler who would use what I learned to harm the family or its olive trees. His suspicions were not unwarranted: tens of thousands of Palestinian olive groves have been destroyed during the fifty years of occupation and many families have been torn apart as a result of Israel's policy of placing Palestinians in jail without a trial. We worked in silence until eventually he spoke to me in Arabic.

'Why are you here? It makes no sense to me. Explain it to me.'

I didn't need to be asked twice. So I spoke with him about the Jewish vision of human rights and dignity and about *tikkun olam*. We were still a few months away from the holiday of Hanukkah, in the darkest time of the year. During this holiday on the first night Jews light one candle. Then the next night

The Little Acts that Tip the Scales

we light two candles and so on for eight nights. I told him that when all was dark you have to light candles.

'Start by lighting that first candle.'

This idea was a revelation to the young man. He got very excited and rushed to tell his family. Now, I'm not naive, I do not know what that young man has done since then. Plenty of people from Palestinian security forces have also been involved in deadly attacks against Israeli civilians. But I believe that because of this encounter there's a much greater chance that this young man will choose a path of non-violence. Although there are no guarantees, the alternative path is full of guarantees: that the only Israelis he will meet will arrest him or attack him. This path is much more likely to lead to bitterness and hatred. In the choice between doing nothing or making sacrifices which can lead us to a better place, for me there is no choice.

For a young Palestinian man to meet an Israeli-Jew, and a rabbi, who is working with them and respecting them does have an impact. It changes their perceptions and expectations of what an Israeli is, and what we can be. In April 2004, I was in the West Bank again helping Palestinians. This time we were planting olive trees. For Palestinians it is a time when they begin to sow the possibilities of a fruitful harvest. Families come together to spend time planting and nurturing the trees that will provide them with an income in the coming months and years, from the thick, yellow oil whose pungency is an unmistakable part of the cookery of both peoples in this conflict.

I was just north of Jerusalem in a town called Biddo participating in a demonstration against the planned route of the separation barrier when I received a call. I was told that the demonstration had turned for the worse with young Palestinian boys firing rocks at the Israeli soldiers. The soldiers had responded by detaining one of the boys and firing tear gas at the others. I turned and ran across the hills hoping to reach the soldiers and pour some water on the flames before it truly exploded.

As I reached the soldiers, through the smoke from the tear gas, I could see a group of Palestinian boys at the bottom of a hill hurling rocks at the army. The soldiers, in turn, were firing rubber bullets back at the boys. Then I noticed a young Palestinian boy tied to the front of a green army jeep, shivering in fear. I ran to comfort him but as I did the commander beckoned me forward, then grabbed me by the throat. I didn't know why I had been arrested but at that point I certainly knew I *was* arrested. Although I tried to protest about my peaceful intentions I was forced to join another Palestinian sent by the worried parents. We were detained and our hands tied behind our back with cable ties. A Swedish journalist was also arrested. Then, we stood and waited – impatiently, for the scene to settle and for the protestors to clear off. When the incident finally came to an end we were all released. The story was reported all over the world and garnered huge media attention: perhaps more than it warranted. (As someone who has spent every waking hour fighting Israeli injustice I am nevertheless opposed to double standards: some people believe that Israel is held to a different standard.) I began to tell some of the journalists bombarding me with questions that they were obsessing over this. It could have happened in many places. Inside, it was very cold comfort for me to say to them, 'Look, in many countries it is as bad, or worse.'

The Little Acts that Tip the Scales

This is my country. It's my people. It's my army. It's my Torah.

The young Palestinian boy, frightened and shaking from his experience, spoke to a fieldworker from the Israeli human rights group B'Tselem, and as he finished describing the horrific events he told the fieldworker that then 'a tall Jewish man in kippah (Jewish head-covering) came and saved me'. Who knows what psychological scars this boy could have for the rest of his life? The work that we do isn't always fun, as a rabbi, as a Jew, as an Israeli, as a human rights defender: it's dangerous. It's not fun to deal every day with the deepest, darkest corners of the country that I love, whether it's fellow Israelis living in poverty, or Palestinians beaten up by Israeli security forces. I've been attacked many times but I will do it again and again for the young boy who will say that a tall Jewish man in a kippah came to his rescue and told him not to be afraid.

In this moment there is enough hope to last me a generation – a young boy traumatised at the hands of the Israeli army understands that it was a Jew who wanted to protect him. If there's going to be any chance for peace, it is I, as an Israeli, particularly a religious Israeli, who – from the Palestinian point of view are all fanatics – can empower Palestinian peacemakers when the average Palestinian says that peace with Israelis is not possible. And they have to empower me when I hear parallel remarks from my fellow Israelis. We must have the sense that we are all in it together. It does help when we speak out, go to court, and lead demonstrations, but there's nothing quite like getting beaten up together for breaking down the stereotypes.

It would be naïve of me to think that the everyday perception Palestinians have towards their Jewish neighbours is positive.

DEFENDING HOPE

Or that most Jews would sacrifice their security to protect a Palestinian, even a child. Our conflict today is fraught with misunderstanding and misperception, grounded in our inability to communicate with each other, to trust each other or to even believe the facts when presented to us.

One of the battlegrounds of this lack of trust and misperception today is in the Negev desert, in the south of Israel. Most Jewish Israelis see the Negev as part of our homeland and believe that the continued development of the desert is a necessary part of Israel's internal growth and development. They are aware that the Negev is populated by Bedouins (Arabic speaking citizens of Israel who, until recent generations, lived nomadic lifestyles).

The Israeli government has created an extensive development plan to attract around a quarter of a million new (Jewish) citizens in to the desert. The government wants to push the focus of development away from the major cities such as Tel Aviv. This will decrease pressure on land usage, lower house prices and create employment in different areas of the country. To achieve this the government is prepared to invest money in the development of the Negev. The financial cost of this development is undoubtedly significant but the social costs are beyond calculation. At risk are the lives of thousands of Bedouin whose entire way of life is threatened by the drive for economic development at all costs. The Bedouins have been organising to resist this exclusive economic development plan through a combination of grassroots organising and legal challenges to the plan.

Among the villages which paid the highest price for this is that of al-Araqib, in the south-central part of the Negev. Looking

The Little Acts that Tip the Scales

east from the hills near to al-Araqib one can see the unleavened land around Gaza and the Israeli port of Ashdod, both sitting on the Mediterranean Sea. Looking west one can see – on a clear day – the land of the Jordan Valley rising and falling in dry sand.

The village of al-Araqib has been demolished more than one hundred times in the past three years. The families who remain there are fighting a series of expulsion orders which will see their homes, and traditional way of life, replaced with a national forest.

Although the Israeli government has sent in police, bulldozers and helicopters to evict the remaining families, they refuse to leave their homes. One leader of the village I have worked closely with is Aziz al-Touri. His son wants to be the first doctor in the village although his pleas and prayers for normalcy have, so far, fallen on stony ground.

The government wants to evict forty thousand Bedouins, like Aziz, from thirteen 'unrecognised' villages and force them into artificial townships. Israeli human rights organisations have teamed up with local Bedouin councils to mount legal challenges against what they describe as potentially the worst human rights catastrophe in forty years. Although the Bedouins represent 30 per cent of the population of southern Israel, they live on less than 3 per cent of the land. If they win their legal battles, they would secure control of an additional 2.5 per cent of the land, in an area which is almost empty.

The Bedouins of the Negev are largely settled communities who rely on agriculture to provide them with a livelihood. The soil, though dry, is fertile and with good access to water can easily be turned productive. However, while Jewish towns in the area are lush and green, the Bedouin villages do not receive proper

DEFENDING HOPE

state services. They often have no water pipes and the Bedouin must walk each day to collect water from trucks and then carry it across the mountains to their homes. In al-Araqib the Jewish National Fund uprooted Bedouin olive trees to plant saplings. Now, every two days, trucks arrive to water the saplings while the Bedouins look on, thirsty. One architect of the Israeli eviction plan has argued that moving the Bedouin will help 'bring them in to the twenty-first century'. However, the evidence shows that those Bedouin who have moved from traditional villages to townships have not fared well. The Bedouin are already among the poorest in our highly unequal state where one-in-five children goes to sleep hungry every night.

But most Israeli-Jews do not see it in this light. Thanks to government tactics involving gross exaggeration and misinformation, 90 per cent of Israeli Jews believe that our fellow Bedouin citizens inside Israel are 'taking over the Negev'. But in a poll conducted by Rabbis for Human Rights, when Jewish Israelis were informed that the outstanding Bedouin land claims amount to only 5.4 per cent of the Negev, the majority believe that this is fair. Yet the misinformation allows the government to plough ahead with the economic development at any price, including the demolition of homes and villages irrespective of the cost to the residents.

/ / /

Five years before I first arrived in Israel a man who was a popular hate figure among many Israelis made a bold move for peace.

The Little Acts that Tip the Scales

I watched the TV coverage of Anwar Sadat's journey to meet with his Israeli counterpart on the American news. The grainy technicolor pictures showed Sadat and his entourage as they stepped from the aeroplane on to Israeli soil. The men in his travelling party look petrified: they know that the decision to visit Israel is full of controversy and fear what price they may pay for it. In the end Sadat's visit was a transformational success. Right up until the moment of his visit Egypt was seen as an enemy state who had been engaged in three wars with Israel since 1948. But the power of Sadat's words, matched by his actions, convinced Israelis that the chance for peace was real. They overwhelmingly supported proposals which the opinion polls showed they had overwhelmingly rejected just a week before. Like Judah they changed. In the end it was threats from inside Egypt which led to Sadat's assassination at the hands of the group known as Islamic Jihad; just as it was, many years later, threats from inside Israel which led to the assassination of Yitzhak Rabin. It is these jihadists and violent, fanatic settlers who receive most of the media attention. But personal experience and opinion polls indicate that the vast majority of Israelis and Palestinians are decent people who aspire to being just and want a better future for their children.

For many years, public opinion polls have consistently shown a sane majority of Israelis and Palestinians who are willing to compromise to achieve a negotiated peace. However, an even larger percentage on both sides say, 'We want peace, but they don't.' This lack of trust characterises each aspect of our relationship as two peoples caught in conflict. Just after Sadat's visit, public acceptance of the current reality changed overnight.

DEFENDING HOPE

Even in the face of acts that make peace more difficult (killings of innocent people) this too can change overnight if a dramatic move could demonstrate that peace was truly within reach.

It would be easy for me to tell Palestinians and Israelis exactly what kind of dramatic move might help. After all our conflict is marked by much drama but mostly of the kind that furthers violence rather than peace. But to do so risks an abrogation of responsibility. My faith teaches me that, like Judah, we must each take responsibility for our actions and the consequences of our decisions.

Most Israelis truly believe we have the most moral army in the world (and we are far from having the most immoral army). To me this belief indicates that Israelis aspire to have the most moral army in the world. In our founding documents we commit to building an Israel:

> based on freedom, justice and peace as envisaged by the prophets of Israel; it will ensure complete equality of social and political rights to all its inhabitants irrespective of religion, race or sex; it will guarantee freedom of religion, conscience, language, education and culture; it will safeguard the Holy Places of all religions; and it will be faithful to the principles of the Charter of the United Nations.

These are the standards we expect of our governments and of our army. We look at other states around the world (the USA, Britain and France) who have faced threats and assess ourselves by the standards of their behaviour. The fact that the behaviour of the US army in Iraq or Vietnam falls far below the expected

The Little Acts that Tip the Scales

standard of international law is not obvious to most Israelis. What they observe is that our army is not so bad compared to the Americans. Palestinians, of course, find this impossible to believe. They see the Israeli army as the one that destroyed their homes in 1948 and in every war subsequent to that. Our role as Israelis, as the more powerful people, is to take extra responsibility for building the trust of our Palestinian neighbours.

A substantial constituency inside Israel can be persuaded to take on that responsibility. Half a million Israelis took to the streets in 2011. Even though the right-wing parties were victorious in the 2015 election campaign, a substantial number of Israelis were concerned about issues of socio-economic justice and wish to halt our lemming march towards a neo-liberal economy in which the government has no responsibility for the poorest and weakest Israelis. Focus groups conducted on behalf of Israeli human rights organisations working in the occupied territories indicate that, while most Israeli Jews care first and foremost about their fellow Jews and believe that almost anything can be justified in the name of our security, they want Palestinians to live and be well.

Being an activist means to have a predilection for beating your head against the wall. Many of my friends and colleagues laugh at me as being one of the last optimists standing. The events of the last years have been a challenge to even my optimism. Yet I ultimately remain hopeful both because of spiritual insights I derive from the Jewish tradition, and because of what I observe around me. I know that my fellow Israelis, and the many Palestinians I have been privileged to know, are basically decent people. While we clearly have a long way to go

DEFENDING **HOPE**

in order to create the society I believe God would have us create, the small successes along the way offer glimpses and reassurances of what is possible.

The question for us, as Jews, tasked with caring for and loving this land, is: have we been destroyers, dispossessors, transferors and oppressors all too often in our short history? Sadly, we have. But the question for us, and for the world who watches Israel's every move so closely, is: is this who we are in our souls? I believe it is not. I think it would be a much more difficult task to turn around an inherently racist and oppressive society. Rather, our task is to say to our fellow Israelis, 'We know that you are decent people aspiring to do the right thing, but look in the mirror.'

In fact, hope increases our responsibility. If there was no chance of improving the situation we could absolve ourselves of responsibility. However, in the Talmud we are taught that all of life is like two perfectly balanced scales. An action of ours that seems meaningless and ineffective at the time could tip the scales one way, or the other. And that's just when you strip away the disinformation so that the soul can be revealed.

Rabbi Eleazar, the son of Rabbi Simeon, teaches that each of us must regard ourselves as if we were half guilty and half meritorious. For each positive act we should be happy to weigh ourselves down in the scale of merit; but for each transgression that we commit woe to us for adding weight on the scale of guilt.

Israelis (and Palestinians) harden their positions because they don't believe that peace is possible. This is the role and importance of hope. It narrows the gap between what seems realistic and what seems possible. When we have faith that ultimately the arc

The Little Acts that Tip the Scales

of history is moving in the right direction, we understand that we may not live to see all of our dreams realised, and that we must do the part that God has ordained for us if they are ever to be realised, even beyond our lifetime. The Torah teaches us how:

> Rabbi Tarfon would say: The day is short, the work is much, the workers are lazy, the reward is great, and the Master is pressing.
> He would also say: It is not incumbent upon you to finish the task, but neither are you free to absolve yourself from it.
> (Pirkei Avot 2:15–16)

We are told many times in the Torah that we must not turn our heads away from the suffering around us. We must pray as if everything depends on God, but act as if everything depends on us, because God helps those who help themselves. When the Israelites were trapped between the Red Sea and Pharaoh's army, they were in a panic. God said to Moses, 'Why are you crying to me? Speak to the Israelites, and tell them to go forward' (Exodus 14:15). The Midrash adds that God did not part the sea until all of the Israelites had jumped into the water. The rabbis debate whether they had to enter up to their necks, or up to their noses. (cf. Babylonian Talmud Sotah 37a). Such is the challenge of building peace – today the Jewish people are resisting each opportunity presented to them to part the waters and create peace between our two peoples. Sadly, the debate is not even focused on whether we should be in a peace process up to our necks or to our noses. The focus is too often on how fast we should move away from the peace process.

DEFENDING **HOPE**

In the midst of such debates I live by the philosophy that says our best effort will produce the results we want to see. Our faith and our folklore are full of such stories. When the Prince has a terrible argument with his parents, and storms out of the palace in anger, his loving parents spend years searching for him. Their messengers finally find him in a far off corner of the kingdom, living as a peasant. He tells the messengers that he has forgotten how to be a prince, and has no strength to return. His parents respond to him by saying, 'Come as far as you can, and we will meet you along the way.' I live with the faith that there are both divine and human forces that will aid us when we make our very best effort. So it must be with Palestinians and Israelis extending to each other a hand that pulls the Other along rather than pushes the Other away.

This is the core principle I apply when building a strategy to resist injustice. I work closely with Palestinians and Israelis to build relationships which, together, can stand firm in the face of violence. These relationships are painful to build, difficult to sustain and often dangerous for people on each side to maintain. Zacharia, the Palestinian fieldworker for Rabbis for Human Rights, who lives and works in Nablus in the north of the West Bank, is no more beloved in his community for working with 'the enemy' than I, as a Jewish rabbi, am beloved by many inside Israel for my work defending Palestinian rights. But by living our daily lives, coherent with our values of non-violence, peace and justice, people begin to develop a certain respect for our integrity.

A Hassidic tale tells of a man lost for days in the forest. He is overjoyed to run into another person, however it turns out that

The Little Acts that Tip the Scales

he too is lost. Nevertheless, they decide that if they compare notes and work together, they will have a greater chance of finding their way. Zacharia and I, alongside the many others who work together, are just such lost people, comparing notes and seeking to find a way out.

Naturally, for Palestinians who experience the brunt of violence and injustice, people want to see the positive impact of our work. Using Israeli lawyers to represent Palestinian farmers in the Israeli courts has created many success stories. Farmers who were once prevented from going near their land – either by military orders or by the violence of settlers – have been given the chance to return to their land.

When people witness positive impact from legal work, grassroots organising and joint work by Palestinians and Israelis they begin to believe in the possibility of change and invest in alternatives to violence. The case for hope is ultimately a matter of faith, backed by experience. These successes may seem small, but they remind us of what is possible, and they mean all the world for those whose lives have been vastly improved. We are taught, and this is repeated in the Qur'an in the name of the Jews, 'One who saves a single life, it is as if one has saved an entire world' (Mishna Sanedrin).

Yes, it is a bit of a burden to always feel that your actions could make a difference, and that you are therefore responsible. And yes, there is an element of swimming upstream. I often feel like I am beating my head against the wall, but I also know that every once in a while the wall breaks. We remember the redemption from Egypt in our daily prayers as a way of maintaining our faith in the redemption yet to come. Jews also traditionally pray every day, 'ashreinu', we are blessed because we are obligated to 'thank and praise and bless and sanctify'. It occurs to me that we are also blessed because we are commanded to maintain hope and do our part to bring closer to reality God's dream for our world.

I think there is something in the human spirit that is stronger than so-called objective reality, especially if it's augmented by the power of God. In both Israel and Palestine, and around the world, there are those who are seeking to increase the sphere of positive influence and to resist the feelings of despair and hopelessness. There are no guarantees in this world: even if we believe that we are doing God's will, we could be wrong. We don't know God's will. We believe, but we don't know. But even if we do not know we should try. There are those that say it is better not to try, because you can screw things up more than you actually can help; but I don't agree with that. I say there's no guarantee we will succeed, but we are certainly not going to succeed if we don't try. The God of the Exodus is the God of possibilities who helped a bunch of slaves to escape from the most powerful empire of the time. That's the power of God, the power of human spirit. Even with that we cannot rely simply on the will of God. We must take our own responsibility and not rely on God, just as each of the Children of Israel had to demonstrate their faith in God before the sea would part for them.

So even if we have faith that God does have a plan for humanity, and for history, it will not happen without our help. We too must move the arc of history towards justice, in God's image. Somewhere down below, things are happening that we don't always know. And I think that what it means is that our

The Little Acts that Tip the Scales

job is not to be rubbing the nose of the naughty puppy in it but rather holding up a mirror, saying we know that you are good, decent people. We know that you strive to be just. We know that some of what we do is scared by our history of oppression, of our own oppression. We know that people who were beaten as children often go on to abuse other children. So, we must say to Israelis: 'We know you want to be good people.' The human soul is essentially good.

Jewish tradition has this wonderful holistic view of life as being two perfectly balanced scales. We never know what little act that may seem meaningless, pointless, irrelevant, ineffective at the time, will be the act to tip the scales one way or the other. This means that you can't ever let down your guard. Just as with the battle for divestment from companies who supported South Africa, it takes time: I did not succeed while I was in university but divestment did eventually happen because the seeds had been planted. We can never know what little act will tip the scales. This reality is a difficult taskmaster because it means that if I have to get up at two in the morning to run down to where some Palestinians are being attacked – when I'd rather do something else – then I will do it. It's a taskmaster, but it's also a source of hope.

The Power of the Powerless

Ghada Ageel

'Hope' is the thing with feathers –
That perches in the soul –
And sings the tune without the words –
And never stops – at all –

...

And sore must be the storm –
That could abash the little Bird
That kept so many warm –

– from "Hope" is the Thing with Feathers' *by Emily Dickinson*

Dedicated to my grandmother, Khadija Ammar, 1925 – October 2016

The story begins in 1948 when Palestinians woke up to a tragedy that distorted their lives forever. Their homes were attacked and around three quarters of a million people (approximately half of the population of historic Palestine) were evicted from their ancestors' lands and forced into exile. Multiple United Nations resolutions condemning this new crisis were issued. Among them was United Nations General Assembly Resolution 194 of 1948, which resolves that 'the refugees wishing to return to their homes and live at peace with their neighbours should be permitted to do so at the earliest practicable date'. Since that

DEFENDING HOPE

point Israel, the state established on the ruins of their homes, rejected and blocked their return. Today, seventy years after that date, millions of displaced Palestinians are still barred from returning home and still live a life of perpetual waiting, enduring multiple hardships in their long exile.

Unable to return to their home, present-day Israel, Palestinians were scattered all over the globe. Hundreds of thousands were obliged to live in great uncertainty about their future in the fifty-nine refugee camps established by the United Nations. My grandmother, Khadija, was one of them. Unable to return to her home in Beit Daras, a village that no longer exists on world maps, Khadija was obliged to live in tragic circumstances in Khan Younis camp, one of Gaza's eight refugee camps, until the day she passed away after sixty-eight years of living in the misery of her circumstances.

Sixty-eight years previously, her life was altered forever when she and her two young children were evicted from their home. Abdelaziz was three and Jawad just one. When her husband, Mohammed, rejoined his family in June 1948, Khadija didn't need to ask about the fate of their home; his eyes answered her question. Beit Daras was no more. Until the day she passed away, sixty-eight years after the expulsion, Khadija remembered the horror of the 1948 dispossession and those unhappy days that followed. She was a witness to a present that was not much different from a tragic past; a past that has cast a dark shadow not only over her life but also over the lives of the generations that followed, stretching across the border of Gaza to Egypt in the south, to Lebanon and Syria in the north, and to Jordan in the east. There are currently over five million Palestinian refugees who, like my grandmother, live a life of perpetual waiting, enduring multiple hardships in their long exile. Once they owned houses, farms and lands, and they enjoyed honour, dignity and hope. Their tale is one of a land that has been emptied of its people and of a people who have been separated from their land and segregated from each other – some never to be reunited. Over 70 per cent of the Palestinian population are refugees whose stories resemble my grandmother's. Either they, or their parents, or grandparents, were driven from their homes in 1948.

As we survey the situation of those refugees today we see them in turmoil. Glimpse the situation of Palestinians in Yarmouk refugee camp in Syria; those locked in the super-maximum prison of the Gaza Strip; those living behind the Apartheid Wall in the West Bank; those Palestinians who are on the run for their lives in Yemen or in Iraq; those stranded on borders; and those risking their lives in the Mediterranean taking death journeys to escape insecurity and find safety for their families. It is the same story: wherever they go Palestinians are forced to flee. It is a continuous Nakba: one of constant suffering with no end in sight.

Today, almost seven decades after the ethnic cleansing, some of the Palestinians born in historic Palestine are still alive and still remember the horror of the 1948 dispossession and those miserable days. The generations who were born after the loss of their homeland – be it under the Israeli military occupation or in exile – and who didn't witness the tragic experiences lived by parents and grandparents, do still retain the story and, to a large extent, the hope of return. In their hearts and minds, the memory of the Nakba is as strong, present and fresh as for those who witnessed it and so are the hopes and dreams that refuse to fade despite the savage winds of war and time.

For Palestinians, these hopes have become over the years a source of empowerment, a form of soft power. It is an active, positive and creative power. If we use it properly, individually or collectively, it could bring about the desired change. I call it the power of the powerless. It is an unusual sort of weapon that could surmount any other form of power as it gives both the mind and the soul a magic lift and charges the body with unusual energy. It is the hidden potency that exists in all humans. It can never fade away unless the individual or the collective let it go.

It is also this force that blends the mind, body and soul for the attainment of any kind of transformation. Hope, therefore, is a multidimensional ideal that pertains to all aspects of human life, including the political. Our national poet Mahmoud Darwish says that 'hope' is the 'incurable disease' of the Palestinian people. Why can we not be cured of this disease? Despite military occupation and exile, there is a greater force which means we hold on to our dreams and demands for rights. People continue to organise politically despite the horrors to which we are still subjected. If this force is hope then can it create the possibility of a just and lasting solution to this most intractable of conflicts?

As a girl in the camp I read a story about two men in a prison cell looking at the outside world. One looked at the mud under his feet. The other looked at the stars in the sky. This is the choice we face as Palestinians.

/ / /

The Power of the Powerless

The Palestinians are an educated people. Two hundred and thirteen thousand students attend forty-nine institutions of higher education. This is remarkable for a small population of around five million people. We lead the Middle East on educational indicators including literacy among women and young people, far surpassing other nations of the developing world in Asia or Africa.

I was no different from many other young women in Palestine, then. I desired an education and saw that it would be a key tool in working for the liberation of my people. So, in 1999 after my studies in the Islamic University I won a scholarship from Exeter University in the United Kingdom to do a master's degree in political science. I was in my late twenties, enthusiastic and full of energy to explore the world. Being in Exeter I had the opportunity to bring the streets of Gaza to my studies. I also had the chance to bring my studies to the streets of Gaza.

One such opportunity came when, over the course of my studies, I interviewed Sheikh Ahmad Yassin, the spiritual founder and leader of Hamas. During the interview Yassin spoke with high eloquence about the future that is going to be ours, the inner strength, the high spirit and the legendary steadfastness of our people. I recall how he argued for the Palestinian need to *hazimat alhazima* or 'defeat the defeat'. At the time Yassin's words seemed to me to be just the empty rhetoric of another man disconnected from reality – like Arafat, who often spoke of 'next year in Jerusalem'. These slogans were scrawled all over the streets of Gaza city and in the walls of my camp:

'THE STRIKE THAT DOESN'T KILL US, STRENGTHENS US.'

DEFENDING HOPE

'THOSE WHO SACRIFICED THEIR SOULS FOR OUR COUNTRY ARE MORE GENEROUS THAN ALL OF US.'

'OUR DAY OF EID IS THE DAY OF OUR RETURN [TO PALESTINE].'

'SMILE, YOU ARE IN GAZA.'

To my mind, then, they were empty slogans and when I met Yassin his words matched them. I argued against his words and ideas with the full force of youth, ending my speech saying that we have not 'defeated the defeat' but rather we are going from one defeat to another defeat. In his response, Yassin was patient and considered. He spoke about the importance of moral legitimacy and rights in winning any battle.

'Hope,' he replied, 'is part of our faith.' He then brought the *Aya* from the Quran saying:

'la taqnatu men rahmit Allah.'
(Never lose hope in the mercy of God.)

Winning, he argued, starts from defeating the defeat in our hearts not to submit to oppression and maintaining our faith in our hearts.

As I left his home, Yassin's words did not mean much to me. But I find these days, whenever I am at the greatest moments of despair, I revisit this conversation. His words about defeating the defeat in our own hearts, about having hope and faith in ourselves, always pop up in the bleakest time and give my soul a lift. Now in the Gaza prison, which follows me around the world no matter where I live, I choose to look at the stars in the sky rather than the mud under my feet.

/ / /

In 2007, just as I was completing my doctorate in the UK, Israel declared Gaza a hostile entity. Then Egypt closed the Rafah Border Crossing – the primary point of exit and entry for the vast majority of Palestinians from Gaza. I could not return to Gaza. With many failed attempts to get back, I immigrated to Canada where I already had family.

During the past nine years living in the Palestinian diaspora, Gaza, my home, has been under constant attack from Israel. The brutal attacks of 2008, 2012 and 2014 left deep scars on my soul and my heart. These were the greatest moments of despair and loss of hope in my life.

There is nothing worse in life than being glued to the TV screen, watching one's nation being slaughtered on an hourly basis, unable to do anything. There is nothing more painful in this universe than hearing the tears and cries of one's mother on the phone and being unable to hug her, to wipe her tears or to comfort her with any words or means. There is nothing more terrifying than living through every night in fear that the coming morning will bring the worst possible news a person can bear, that a member of one's immediate family has been killed. And last, but not least, there is nothing more horrible on this globe than something happening to a family member when he or she is barred from returning to his or her family and home.

DEFENDING HOPE

As I watched the attacks in 2014, I felt the same sense of despair as I had watching them in 2008. But now I felt even more strangled. I was not alone. Many people, namely Palestinians in exile, but also activists and solidarity groups, as well as Muslims at large, were feeling crushed watching the mass murder of civilians and the devastation of Palestinian infrastructure that scaled new heights in this aggression. They felt Gaza and wept for it deeply.

The aggression was getting more brutal and so was the feeling of being devastated and broken – blended all together. Together with solidarity groups, we mobilised, advocated, demonstrated, wrote, gave interviews and tried to imagine new ways to bring this injustice to the forefront of the Western popular imagination in the belief that this would help it to stop. For me this is part of my being as a Palestinian born in Gaza's camps. My family and community were under attack. So, as an academic teaching political science, as an activist whose role is to mobilise energies and advocate for just causes, as a writer who attempts to report and voice the suffering, and finally as a woman and a mother who is aware of the specific and very heavy burdens that women bear in this chain of horrific events. Each of these descriptions to the self is different, at least in part. And each is important, at least to me.

I was glued to computer and TV screens following the live news of the aggression minute by minute. Like many of the diaspora Palestinians, I felt it over my skin and deep in my bones. At the same time, I was trying to stay focused, to do what I needed to do to support Gaza. In all of this I wanted to look for any way to get me out of the state of despair that started to take over and at the same time look for any sort of light, somewhere, somehow: to keep going.

The Power of the Powerless

With the start of the ground invasion on 18 July 2014, the civilian death toll became enormous. My ill, octogenarian grandmother asked my uncle that in the event of her death he would dig a hole and bury her under the mulberry tree by her home in the camp. She was very specific that he should not bury her in the family cemetery. She was all too aware that the cemetery is often hit by the bombs from US-supplied F-16s. In that cemetery, there is no dignity, even in death. The aggression was unbelievable, an aggression towards a helpless, imprisoned, besieged, starved and occupied population. It was an attack on a civilian population including women and children. Israel killed on average ten children a day, every day for the fifty-one days of the operation.[1] It was an attack on the Palestinian infrastructure. Israel targeted UN schools and shelters, hospitals, clinics, mosques, homes, centres for disabled people and water wells. There was no safe place for people to run to. On the contrary, safe, sacred and supposed-to-be protected places were subject to attack; not in a single incident but continuously: the safe havens were the targets.

For me, the attack was broader than all of that. It was an attack on human liberty, on international law, on the right to life, right to work, to move and have a safe place to access basic humanitarian essentials. It was an attack on all of us no matter where we are: an attack on all humanity. All that we got in the face of this attack were empty words of condemnation. Such words ensure that Israel feels impunity and will continue to carry out such attacks over and over again – as it has done in history.

By the end of July, with the attack on Khuza'a, a village east of Khan Younis, and the UN school in Jabaliya camp, I started

DEFENDING HOPE

to lose my ground. I felt, perhaps for the first time ever, that the store of hope that keeps me running was gone. I could no longer feel – as I always have – that I just have to continue doing whatever I do, trying whatever I try, along with many friends, colleagues, partners and others who I don't even know, because at some point, some time, things will have to change and justice must prevail. The inhumanity will have to end. I listened to the words of the UNRWA commissioner general after the UN designated shelter was attacked for the sixth time. He said killing children in their sleep 'is an affront to all of us, a source of universal shame. Today the world stands disgraced.' I, too, felt that shame. Even worse, I started to feel that I was becoming part of that distant cruel and complicit world that offers Palestinians only words; words which though probably not empty, are still only words.

By early August I felt as if earth lost its gravity. Or in other words I felt my body lost its gravity to earth. I was shattered and scattered into small fragmented pieces and sprinkled in the air. I felt I was unable to give any more talks or participate in any demonstrations. I was not only burnt out but I also ran out of hope – to a point beyond return and, seemingly, beyond repair. Despite my relentless attempts to look for hope amid this nightmare, or even search for possible ways to help myself out of it, I kept sinking into a state of greater despair.

I desperately needed to be back to the ground, and just not any ground. Only one ground can gather my scattered body and my soul. It was Gaza. I took the decision and I booked my tickets.

The questions I confronted during the 2014 aggression were many. How could I, as one of the diaspora, challenge the state of myself and the collective feeling of powerlessness? How could I continue carrying a torch for myself, for people around me and more importantly for the people in the slaughterhouse? I wondered what options I had to restore my self and rise from the state of despair that impaired my vision and swallowed me. But how? After all, how many good alternatives do hopeless people have? Right from the beginning of the attack I kept looking for options to restore my broken self and spirit. But there was nothing I could find. I was surrounded by blackness. I kept looking for a different approach to interpret events, bloodshed and massacres. I kept chasing the hidden parts of the picture that I might have missed, as had happened in that conversation with Yassin back in early 2000. But the state of despair blocked my sight. I was impaired and I wanted my sight back.

I decided I must return to Gaza. I needed to be beside my people in the pain and the trauma, the horror and the scarring fear. I wanted to grieve with them. Returning to Gaza would also allow me to defy my own state of powerlessness by eliminating the defeatist approach that had begun to take over. In choosing hope against defeat, I was defying the state of despair. I was fighting for existence. Hope became my *modus vivendi*. I could stand upright and resist or I could choose to sink into the defeat. I knew deep in my heart that this path of defeat would lead to my permanent internal subjugation. Put boldly, I opted to defeat my defeat. Finally, by going to Gaza, I sided with an epic struggle, one that has very clear-cut lines between justice and injustice, between the right side of history and the wrong one. Despite all these decisions I remained uncertain about whether this would have the desired impact.

DEFENDING HOPE

On 8 August 2014 I left Canada for Gaza. My family and my friends begged me not to go. But the words of Dr Martin Luther King Jr kept echoing in my mind: 'There comes a time when one must take a position that is neither safe, nor politic, nor popular, but he must take it because conscience tells him it is right.' It was not merely a position but rather a decision that could cost my life. I felt King's words deeply and did act on what I felt right at that point in time when Gaza was a slaughterhouse.

The minute I stepped into Gaza I felt I was back in my orbit. I started to sense some gravity and my feet started to touch my inner ground. From the very first day, I joined my sisters-in-law, neighbours and the armies of volunteers of my camp in Khan Younis helping the displaced at the United Nations schools. Around two hundred and forty-five thousand newly 'refugeed' refugees – one in seven Palestinians in Gaza – were forced out of their homes into UN facilities. The schools were unable to cope with the volume of people and, therefore, the people in my refugee camp offered shelter and food to these victims, some displaced for the third, fourth or perhaps even fifth time. With no electricity, most of Gaza went back to candlelight. It was the living proof that it is better to light a candle than curse the darkness. Similarly, there was little water and thin resources but grand people with a strong passion to help. Neighbours shared medicine with one another so as to ensure that they would live to see the end of the offensive. This sense of solidarity and the principle of protecting neighbours through thick and thin, and the resolution not to be dispossessed again, undoubtedly played a part in the massacre at the Kwari' family home when

The Power of the Powerless

neighbours did not flee the targeted home but massed to it in defiance of the Israeli missile attack that soon levelled the home with total disregard for human life.

Neighbours also gladly shared jokes throughout the war. Humour kept us going. I recall one young man who worked in the tunnels. These tunnels are the lifeline of people in Gaza. Built to defy Israel's siege imposed on the Strip, they provide citizens with some of the products of ordinary life, like food, medicine and cigarettes. Working in the tunnels is a dangerous job because there is always the risk of collapse – even more so during times of war. This young man told me one day before he set off for work, 'If I come back you are invited to have tea in my house in Rafah.' I was happy to receive this invitation. 'But', he continued, 'if I do not come back you are invited to have coffee in my house at Rafah.' He smiled before setting off: coffee is what they serve at funerals.

I am happy to report that I drank tea with him in Rafah, but many coffees were drank at the funerals of young men lost while working in tunnels, putting their lives in danger to rescue other lives from starvation, in defiance of the words of Dov Weisglass, adviser to Ehud Olmert, the Israeli prime minister of the day, 'The idea is to put the Palestinians on a diet, but not to make them die of hunger.' With each cup of tea I drank during the sixteen days of aggression and raining death from the sky I witnessed in Gaza, I recalled the young man's words and his sense of humour. It was during these bleak days that I lost my appetite for my favourite drink, coffee. I have no rational explanation for such dietary change, except a solidarity and resistance act of my body with the state I lived amid the war.

DEFENDING HOPE

During the eight days of ceasefire (11–19 August), people ran from funeral to funeral, from shock to shock, from tragedy to tragedy in a deeply connected community. There was no time for grief and no time for tears. They were living in impossible conditions – made worse by the lack of every basic element needed to live and despite that they were doing the undoable all while expecting death at any moment. The state of being paralysed, and of self-loss, was buried amid the work with relatives and neighbours in the camp, ordinary people, men and women of different ages, who toiled endlessly with smiles on their faces. I followed them closely and joined in on their jokes and so began to gather strength in my self.

If they somehow manage – in spite of everything they've witnessed and experienced and lived through – to hold on to hope and the faith, then it's definitely there. And for me as well. I started to feel my soul return to my body with the collective spirit. I started to regain my self. I started to feel my soul back by knowing and feeling, tasting and learning with the people in my camp. In these two final weeks of war on Gaza came the moment of my redemption.

When the temporary nine-day ceasefire fell apart on 19 August uncertainty dominated. We had around a week more of horror and trauma, a continuation to the fifty-one days of death and destruction. The strength of community I witnessed in this difficult time, however, epitomises the meaning of the word 'hope'.

Upon my return to Canada, and amid vivid memories of barbarism and scarring fears, I started to think about the diaspora's role in keeping the cause and the hope alive, about how to best place the Palestinian voices, views and narratives – especially those of women – at the heart of the discourse. I started to think about the two million people I left behind and how I can effectively help them. I started to think about their story, one of legendary resistance and great resilience that has no limit, one with grave human rights abuses, of denial and oppression. I started to think about getting back to basics when looking at Palestine: the country, the story, the once-upon-a-time beauty, the people (both the collective and the individuals). I also started to think about the hopes and dreams for change, and the work needed to make them come true.

The positive energy I gained while in Gaza was a fantastic source of light and helped me bit by bit to get back to sort of semi-normality. My book of essays about the reality of apartheid in Palestine was due to be published. I knew this could tell part of the story, returning it to the root causes: the continued catastrophes, resulting from the original catastrophe of 1948. I want to offer an explanation to people seeking to understand the most recent aggression on Gaza and provide an urgent and critical analysis of the causes of the immense destruction in the Strip in 2014.

Many sleeves need to be rolled to make the desired change and to retain the hope. On my part, the strategy is to 'write for rights' by continuing the rights-based approach I take in my research. I hold that indigenous voices are a vital constituency for peacemaking: giving indigenous people a central say is a prerequisite in credible research efforts. Palestine is a hot and contentious subject, and it requires a growing, up-to-date knowledge base. By shedding light on the injustices of exile and dispossession audiences can understand the absence of a dignified future for Palestinians.

The Palestinian voice is missing from, or deformed in, the mainstream media narratives, especially in North America. If I can show the great work going on it may create a movement of people who will stand up to governments and ask them to act to stop what is happening in the name of justice.

2014 was a turning point, a strong shaking and awakening to the self and to the collective in and outside historic Palestine. The impact of the 2014 attack on Gaza is like that of the Arab awakening (dubbed by commentators as the 'Arab Spring'). Both events broke the barriers of fear, helplessness and hopelessness and freed the captive souls to look for redemption. Lots of work still needs to be done but the first step has been taken.

Also, the brutality of the Israeli attack of 2014 has reminded the people of the injustice of the occupation, the justice of the Palestinian struggle and the efforts that needed to be invested in order to help justice prevail. It strengthened the attachment of diaspora Palestinians to their homeland and opened the doors wide for the youth to join the solidarity campaigns and activism. The brutality has also pushed many, including diaspora Palestinians, to abandon their mute state and to actively espouse the Palestinian cause. By crossing all the lines, Israel aimed to send Palestinians everywhere a message of humiliating defeat. This strategy backfired and many of those in the diaspora have come forward, devoting mind and heart to their struggle, and circumventing the occupation's attempt to sideline the Palestinian cause.

The scepticism about what direction should be taken no longer exists. People started to show up in significant numbers to events and to demonstrations, mobilising and campaigning for Palestine, sending messages – letters, emails – urging governments to take a stand. They became better aware of the necessity to build awareness. They started to realise the importance of engagement and mobilisation and its impact on the policy-makers. Hundreds of thousands of people went into the streets protesting, in fact if we add the numbers together we are talking about millions of people who took to streets protesting the injustice and the slaughter. I think the revolutions in the EU parliaments symbolically voting to recognise a Palestinian State in 2014/2015 should be read in the context of this huge public advocacy and support for justice in Palestine.

One of the key tools activists have used is that of boycott, divestment, sanctions (BDS). This is a non-violent strategy aiming to ensure Israeli compliance with international law and in support of Palestinian rights. The movement is a joint appeal from one hundred and seventy Palestinian civil society organisations that was launched in 2005. The goals of the movement are:

1) An end of the occupation of Arab land;
2) Equality of all citizens of Israel;
3) The right of return of the Palestinian refugees.

BDS has resuscitated the Palestinian national movement as a tool open to all for participation – each one in their own way and appropriate for their own context. The rapid response to this rights-based movement has resulted in a global movement and global actions. Since its inception and all through the past eleven years, BDS groups have been formed in every major city in Europe and North America.

Dozens of international actions, endorsements, statements and letters are calling on international civil society to support BDS against Israel until the rights of the Palestinians are respected. The support for such rights is steadily growing across university campuses everywhere. BDS is without doubt a major event in the history of Palestinian mobilisation. This unprecedented international solidarity with Palestine and huge steps forward for the BDS movement are providing activists with hope and reassuring them that the strategy adopted to scuttle the occupation is the right one.

The 2014 vote of the 1.8 million strong Presbyterian Church in the United States in favour of divesting $21 million from three corporations linked with Israel's military (Caterpillar, Hewlett Packard, and Motorola) was a huge success for BDS. A European Union directive explicitly excluding Israeli colonies in the West Bank (including East Jerusalem) from all future agreements between the EC and Israel is an indication that states too are starting to take their responsibilities seriously. The directive covers all areas of cooperation with Israel, including economics, science, culture, sports, and academia.

The Bill Gates Foundation, the largest private foundation in the world, divested from G4S. A petition signed by more than fourteen thousand people and demonstrations outside the Gates Foundation offices in London, Johannesburg and Seattle called on the Gates Foundation to divest from G4S because of its role in providing equipment and services to prisons where Israel detains and tortures Palestinian political prisoners.

The Power of the Powerless

BDS is a significant tool for activists because it allows them to organise, to break the silence experienced at the elite level and to take practical steps. It answers the questions raised by human rights activists and those of free conscience as to what can be done to support Palestinians. It offers everyone a way to voice their protest within the means they can, from wherever they reside. BDS in all its forms – academic, economic, cultural, sport – is becoming the global answer to a question that aims to shake the conscious of the world. It is part of the politics of hope and not the politics of despair that has spread among Palestinians and activists alike after the failure of Oslo. In fact, it is a counter tool to that politics of disappointment which strangles the local and the global masses. Now we have an opportunity to work together to have a unified stance, one that complies with human rights and international law.

BDS is also a strong sign of the unity of humanity towards each other. It calls on us all to be citizens of the world who not only care but who also act to end injustice. When people talk to each together, learn from each other and explore and develop alternatives, they are creating emerging hope for Palestinians and for humanity.

Positive action creates a sense of progress (and hence hope) even if such progress takes time. It's the action, the right action, that matters here. This action, however small, sends a message of hope to the oppressed people on the ground. Human rights defenders are aware that it may not be in their power as people to change the world or that it may not be in their time that there'll be any actual result. But that doesn't mean they stop doing the right thing. Doing nothing only contributes to the

DEFENDING HOPE

state of powerlessness and will not bring any change or bring us closer to justice.

Palestinians are successfully moulding the concept of hope into a revolutionary tool in their battle for dignity and freedom. We are trying to spread this incurable disease as widely as we can. The power of the truth is a revolutionary strategy of resistance.

My grandmother, a true tower of resistance, passed away on 16 October 2016. She was buried in Khan Younis refugee camp in the family cemetery and not in Beit Daras, the village from which she had been expelled sixty-eight years earlier. She lived a harsh and often cruel life, struggling through poverty and the humiliation of losing everything overnight. Despite this she was a gentle soul, always full of kindness and stories. She was always a true tower of resilience and strength. It was impossible to interact with her and leave empty handed, despite having little to spare herself.

May I be half the person she was in the face of adversity. We, her descendants, hope to be buried in Beit Daras, the village of her childhood, having lived a full life, with equal rights. In this, we hope.

Note

1. Andrew Marszel, 'Children killed in Gaza during 50 days of conflict', *The Daily Telegraph*, 26 August 2014. www.telegraph.co.uk/news/worldnews/middleeast/gaza/11056976/The-children-killed-in-Gaza-during-50-days-of-conflict.html/.

This Life Goes Out to the World Through Our Lenses

Joanne O'Brien

Sometimes recording the aftermath of violence and terror, of destruction and desolation is all that can be done. Powerful events have taken place; the photographer is only an observer and must accept that they cannot change what has happened. They have two choices: they could turn away, not engage, and focus elsewhere, for the pain of the injured is hard to witness; or they can listen to the traumatised, and by their presence and by respectful photography attempt to offer some comfort. This work is costly for the photographer on a psychological, let alone material level. It can be desolate, chiefly because they are aware that all the empathy in the world cannot set right the wrong. They are constantly aware that imagination, which sustains the ability to empathise, cannot contend with the unimaginable. A lurking sense of potential personal failure requires hope in mitigation; a sense that, at sometime in the future, the images produced will have a use and a value as evidence, whether legal or historical. This chapter looks at the work of five photographers and two videographers who work in the occupied territories of Palestine. How does their work contribute to the defence of Palestinian human rights? How do they overcome the many personal challenges they encounter? What is the role of hope in this work?

Historically, social documentary and journalistic photography have been used as tools for social and political change. One early

DEFENDING HOPE

exponent was Jacob Riis, a Danish immigrant to the United States. In 1887 he set about documenting the housing poverty and squalor endured by recent immigrants to New York. He gave lectures using lantern-slides of his photographs and published a book in 1890 called *How the Other Half Lives*. He took advantage of new developments with flash lighting to document the dark and squalid living conditions.

Technical innovation has often been an engine for new departures and ways of working in photography. The widespread use of digital photography, and the advent of the World Wide Web opened up many new opportunities for the production of images and their distribution. All of the people under discussion here have taken advantage of this new technology, which has significantly altered how they might access an audience and disseminate news and information about the struggle for human rights in the West Bank and Gaza. Their capacity to reach their audience is predicated on the existence of electronic imagery in the form of digital photography, whether still images or video. They all focus on how Palestinians experience and resist the Israeli occupation and colonisation. Like the early pioneers, their work often straddles journalism and social documentary photography. As we shall see, for one group of photographers, technology has also made it possible to develop a new paradigm for working on human rights issues.

'WE ARE STILL HOPING THAT PEOPLE WILL CHANGE AND THIS IS THE HOPE THAT DRIVES US TO CONTINUE.'[1] *Anne Paq*

This Life Goes Out to the World Through Our Lenses

For the photographers and videographers, whom I look at here, the practice of photography offers them the possibility of expressing their hope for the future, by bravely confronting the existing repression. They do their work in the spirit of self-expression and the search for peace and justice. The very act of photography can be a gesture of hope for the future, both in the short and long term. At the most basic level, taking a photograph or recording a video can be a simple act of solidarity; bearing witness in the hope that this will somehow contribute to justice eventually being done. The act of pressing a shutter release betokens both a sense of being in the moment and of imagining a future. Photography can provide evidence for the potential judgement of future generations, both in an historical and in a legal sense. Recording images of struggle and oppression is one way of contributing to the search for better times. The innumerable photographers/citizen journalists in the occupied territories of Palestine offer their own view. This challenges the dead-end narrative perpetrated by the Israeli authorities (with the collusion of some elements of the international media) who portray themselves and their state as victims of the irrational and violent Arabs. Digital technology enables photographers to offer a plurality of views on what is taking place.[2]

The Israelis understand this and use physical intimidation, arrest and imprisonment in their attempts to censor images and reports of what is taking place under their military occupation. Israeli citizens are actually legally forbidden from visiting much of the West Bank and Gaza, and must actively look behind the headlines if they want to know what is happening only a few miles away in the West Bank/occupied Palestinian territories

(OPT).³ There, the Palestinian population live under military occupation by the Israeli Defence Forces (IDF). This is part of what Ariella Azoulay has eloquently described as the 'framework of control' whereby three and a half million people are denied any political status.⁴

There are many passionate filmmakers and photographers doing important and useful work in Palestine, but unfortunately there is only space here to discuss a representative sample.⁵ I will examine the work of seven people: two videographers and five photographers (some of whom also shoot video).⁶ Five are Palestinian, one is Israeli and another is French. What kinds of situations do these photographers cover and what are their working conditions?

First and foremost, they are working in a militarised environment, where uneasy peace frequently erupts into outright conflict. Unsurprisingly, images of violence and protest frequently reach the pages and screens of media organisations covering the occupied territories of the West Bank and Gaza. However, a common aim of these photographers is to capture images of the day-to-day difficulties faced by Palestinians living under military occupation, in what remains of their country. Anne Paq voices a view shared by them all:

> If there was an outburst of violence [it gets covered] and we will see [pictures of] kids throwing stones. But I don't think people really grasp what it means to live under military occupation. General documentation of daily life in Palestine is usually missing from the media. This is what I have been trying to do. This is the paradox of Israel/Palestine;

This Life Goes Out to the World Through Our Lenses

it is swamped by so many journalists, photographers and cameramen, and still we are missing the point. It is really hard to describe, it's not very sexy for the media, the daily humiliation of the Palestinians under military occupation.

Daily life is subject to severe physical constraints; the Israeli-built Separation Wall cuts a swathe through Palestinian farmland and villages, separating neighbours and family members. Travelling even a short distance for any reason, whether for work, education, health or leisure, is frequently difficult and unpredictable because of long detours due to road closures. Any journey can become very fraught because it is subject to the whim of bored young Israelis at checkpoints, who are doing their military service. Local resident and photographer Abed Quisini sees his work as, 'part of a struggle for dignity in life'. As he explains:

> I am living in Nablus, even on my days off maybe I'll be stuck at the checkpoint with my family. My car will be searched and [then] I'll take pictures of the army searching my car.[7]

Living conditions are characterised by a continual and pervasive sense of threat and domination of Palestinians by armed Israelis enforcing military law.[8] This military 'framework of control' is a major cause of socio-economic deprivation, which has been described as 'regime-led disaster'. It creates living conditions that while stopping short of catastrophe can be easily mistaken for everyday poverty.[9] In besieged Gaza, for example, there are chronic electricity shortages following the bombing by the Israelis of the electricity generating station in 2014.[10] Samar Abu

DEFENDING HOPE

Elouf has documented how everyday life there has been affected by the Israeli bombardments, especially for women:

> I took photos of how people lived during a power outage without gas and how they cooked with fire. I focused on women, what they [must] do when there is a power cut.[11]

In Hebron and elsewhere, B'Tselem's volunteer videographers record the constant arbitrary difficulties faced by Palestinians at Israeli checkpoints. They also regularly film incidents of very young children playing in the street, who are suddenly taken into military custody and questioned about alleged stone throwing, as a means of frightening and shaming the child.[12]

Palestinians also face innumerable bureaucratic regulations and may not build or extend their homes, so villages and towns cannot expand naturally, and have become chronically overcrowded.[13] By contrast, the continual encroachment on Palestinian land by Jewish settlers, for whom the Israeli state is building large towns in the countryside, has been a constant aspect of life under occupation for decades. For example, the village of Bil'in has a population of around one thousand eight hundred and the population of the nearby Jewish settler city of Modi'in Illit is over sixty-four thousand.[14] Across the valley from the village, the huge white conurbation gleams incongruously in the rural setting. Established in 1994, the settlement was built on land taken from five Palestinian villages including Bil'in. In many parts of the occupied territories, Palestinian farmers face armed fundamentalist Jewish settlers who attempt to intimidate them and steal their farmlands. The

This Life Goes Out to the World Through Our Lenses

IDF backs them up as they flout the law.[15] In 2005 in Bil'in, the building of the Separation Wall led to the loss of half of the village's agricultural land. However, in 2011, after a campaign of peaceful weekly demonstrations and legal actions, the villagers won back six hundred and fifty dunams of the one thousand nine hundred and fifty that had been confiscated.

Hamde Abu Rahma lives in Bil'in. In 2009 he started to photograph life there under military occupation, after his cousin Bassem Abu Rahma was killed by the IDF whilst taking part in one of the peaceful weekly village demonstrations protesting the loss of their land.[16] He felt impelled to give up his business studies and take up photography:

> In my work I try to talk about the life and the occupation. I focus on settlements, walls, Israelis, checkpoints – the real problem for the people right now.[17]

The everyday privations of a life under occupation are Hamde's focus. Like many in Bil'in, his family has suffered as a result of participating in the protests. Apart from his cousin who was killed in 2009, his brother, Kumis Abu Rahma was injured in the head by a plastic bullet and was in a coma for a month; it took him two years to recover. Then a sister of his cousin Bassem, Jawaher, died from tear gas inhalation in 2010. He sees himself as activist first and photographer second:

> I have to do something that supports Palestine but won't make me a terrorist. [So I decided] I'll start documenting what they're doing. People have to see this. They may come

to destroy my house and my family. I have to do something legal to keep them away from me.

In his book, *Roots Run Deep*, he looks at everyday life under military occupation. He records aspects such as the loss of grazing land for livestock, or the awful consequences of constant exposure to tear gas.[18] The Bil'in villagers' campaign has been reported widely and has received some Israeli and international support. In response, the IDF conduct frequent night raids on the village. Photographing these army incursions is dangerous work. Hamde finds that the soldiers are often very jumpy and trigger-happy. But, despite the threats of violence, he does it out of a sense of duty:

> What I'm doing – it's putting me in a dangerous place. Many times I think that I don't want to go. I always tell myself that the next time, I'm not going ... but I never want to feel like I'm a coward.

While Hamde Abu Rahma is motivated by a sense of loyalty to his own community, what impels both Haim Schwarczenberg and Anne Paq is an outsider's objection to the immorality of the Palestinian's situation and identification with their cause. Israeli photographer Haim Schwarczenberg has been documenting the struggle of Nabi Saleh villagers against the loss of their land.[19] Based in Tel Aviv, he was an animal rights activist for more than fifteen years before he became interested in Palestinian issues. In 2010 he started asking questions about the military occupation in the West Bank and after going on a tour of Hebron organised by Breaking the Silence, he was very shocked by what he saw.[20]

A couple of months later he documented a Palestinian solidarity demonstration in Jerusalem, then he decided to go and see the situation for himself in Bil'in and Nabi Saleh.[21] 'I started meeting Palestinian people [in order] to get to know them.' He considers himself an activist photographer:

> I know that my opinion is more leftist than the majority of Israelis. I've tried to bring Israeli people, even Zionists, to Nabi Saleh to see what we are doing [there]. And I saw many of them change their minds.[22]

Like many progressive Israelis, Haim laments how the historical legacy of the Holocaust had been used politically, to inculcate fear and suspicion as the basis for the country's political culture.

> The feeling that we get here in Israel [is that] we always need to be afraid we will lose the state we worked so hard to get … Growing up in fear that we're surrounded by enemies and we have to fight all the time to keep our place.

However, he became very despondent at the response of other Israelis to the 2014 military operation against Gaza, and started to feel that Israelis suffer from a kind of willful political myopia:

> The curious thing is that even if you open their minds and they see the reality is different than what the media, or the educational system, teaches them, even then, if an Israeli gets killed, it's like they didn't see anything at all. I think that most Israelis support Palestinian rights as long as it does not affect

their rights. Then came the war in Gaza … You [could] see the writings on Facebook against the Palestinians. Then I told myself that I'm not wasting my time anymore with Zionists.

Instead of trying to change the minds of other Israelis, Haim decided to focus on 'the outside world'. He avails of digital platforms to publish his work and uses Facebook and YouTube to highlight Palestinian resistance and Israeli solidarity protests. He started his blog in 2011 with a story from Bil'in about the weekly protest against the Separation Wall.[23] Then he began to photograph the protests at Nabi Saleh every week. In December 2011, he photographed the death of Mustafa Tamimi (cousin of Ahed Tamimi) from a tear gas canister fired directly at his head. His images were used as evidence of the illegal targeting and killing of the young protestor (see fig. 15). However, the IDF decided not to prosecute the Israeli soldier involved. Haim was badly affected after witnessing Tamimi's death, and by the subsequent lack of any prosecution. He wrote about his depression on his blog, believing that it was important to be open about the sense of horror that he experienced:

> I know a lot of Palestinian activists and photographers that experience trauma and post-trauma. It's something that we don't speak about and I think that we should. For that reason, after the case of Mustafa [Tamimi] I wrote about my experience. I felt that it made me strong[er]. I don't have a problem to speak about it even if I speak about it in an intimate way.[24]

This Life Goes Out to the World Through Our Lenses

He continued to cover demonstrations in Nabi Saleh and he is clear about his reasons:

> [Firstly] I could take part in a different struggle but I feel connected to these people. And the army, they act differently when they see cameras. My second reason is to show what's happening to everyone in the world. I have actually followed this demonstration for more than four years, every week. I have an archive [of the struggle]. Lastly if something happens, I can be there as a photographer; if there is a situation then I can capture it, like Mustafa [Tamimi's death].

He has a sense of recording history and like other photographers he feels that the presence of cameras can inhibit the army violence:

> The army, they act differently when they see cameras. I've been to one demonstration over half a year ago in the evening, [where] only the people in the village went out, so the soldiers started to shoot live bullets. Usually they use tear gas and rubber bullets. They don't care. So for sure the camera lowers the [level of military] violence.

He also regularly covers the small Palestinian solidarity movement protests in Israel, and what he terms 'social justice' protests. For example, the shortage of housing for working class Palestinian families in Jaffa (close to Tel Aviv) is a big issue. In October 2011 Haim captured on video the brutal beating and eviction of a Palestinian man, Samer Kassem, from a run-down

DEFENDING **HOPE**

property that he and his homeless family had occupied after their previous home, a tent, had caught fire. The video has had nearly one hundred and fifty thousand views.[25] Despite giving a copy of his damning footage to the police investigation, he never heard from them and the case was closed. He supplies photographs free of charge to publications in order to publicise the injustices he sees:

> [With] Israeli magazines and media, if you ask for money they will not publish. The thing that leads me is to expose the struggle. The money doesn't count. I do it as an activist.

Haim feels that there is currently less hope in Israel for progressive solutions to the country's problems because of the extremely right-wing government, which has held power since 2009. Yet he remains hopeful for the long-term:

> I feel that things will change, for sure. When you look at history there is not a fascist regime that stayed. It may [take] ten years or fifty years. On [the] one hand ... people keep suffering and it keeps getting worse all the time. But on the other hand the actions of the government show that it is afraid and maybe [that is] a sign of the beginning of the end of this [repression] policy, which gives me a sense of hope.

French-born Anne Paq also sees herself as an activist photographer. In 2003 she came to Palestine to work with the human rights organisation, 'Al Haq'. She was set on a career in the legal profession when she was drawn to photography and realised how much potential it had for furthering work on human rights:

> I saw the immediate impact that photos can have on people ... that was a fantastic support [for being able] to share the story.

Her first piece of photographic work in Palestine was an exhibition on the widespread practice of collective punishment of Palestinians by the Israeli authorities. She went on to develop another photography project, *Images for Life*, with teenagers at the Alrowwad Centre in the Aida Refugee Camp; empowering Palestinians to use photography and video has been a core aspect of her work. In 2006 she was invited to become a member of the photographers' collective, 'Activestills', a group of Israeli, Palestinian, and international photographers committed to progressive social and political change in Palestine/Israel and to supporting the boycott, divestment and sanctions campaign. They explicitly support the ideal of social justice and question the idea of journalistic objectivity. They came together in 2005 as a response to the highly biased coverage in the Israeli media towards the Palestinian unarmed and popular struggle against Israeli military occupation of Gaza and the West Bank. They see the Israeli state as founded on the notion of the separation of different communities and layers of society, the Separation Wall being a striking example of this policy.

Like Haim Schwarczenberg, Anne Paq has a similar perspective on the inter-relatedness of the issues she covers:

DEFENDING **HOPE**

In Activestills, we believe that the struggles are all inter-related. We work on different issues. It is not only about Palestine, it is about LGBTQ rights, it is about animal rights.[26]

She feels that things have changed for the better in the last ten years as more citizen-journalists have got involved:

> When Activestills started, we were basically almost the only ones going to the demonstrations as activists, documenting the struggle and the really horrible repression by the army. There was us and the photographers working with [the news] agencies and media. Over the years we have witnessed such a change. Now, on a demonstration there are maybe twenty Palestinian photographers with their phones, [still] cameras, video cameras, documenting every aspect of the demonstrations and putting it on Twitter, Facebook and YouTube, almost live. It is fascinating and is really important because everything is documented. So, when the Israeli army comes up with many lies, then you have the image that can establish the truth. And it's important because, when the Israeli army enter the villages at night, [the villagers] go out and film … when we cannot be there.

Despite a difficult and sometimes heart-wrenching working environment, she remains focused and optimistic:

> I'm an optimist, I think people can change. Even if at times it is hard to assess the effects of your work … it is important to carry on doing it. This is something that I will do regardless.

This Life Goes Out to the World Through Our Lenses

She believes in the capacity of photography to tell stories, often in just one frame (see fig. 14):

> For instance, I have a very strong photo of Bethlehem checkpoint at 5 a.m. when you can see a line of people, Palestinian workers, just next to the apartheid wall and you can see them totally squeezed into that corridor next to the wall, it's horrible. Anyone with a bit of sensitivity can see there is something very wrong there; why do these Palestinians have to queue everyday in such conditions? This is very degrading and I think that you feel that from the photo … The power of photography is that you show this is reality happening – in one frame.[27]

Anne's work has been widely published and exhibited. She has also worked a great deal in Gaza since 2010. As she got to know the place, she realised that there was more to it than the problems caused by the siege. In 2012 she shot a video about artists and alternative sub-cultures in Gaza, *Not a Dreamland*.[28]

> I discovered … a very creative scene and young people doing things just to enjoy themselves. I managed to meet a lot of people doing hip hop, [some] break-dancers, artists and young people doing parkour. This is what you want to show, a complex picture of a place. It's a society with all its paradoxes, its greatness and weakness facing a very difficult situation, being oppressed [and] at the same time resisting in so many different ways, in so many inspiring ways.

DEFENDING **HOPE**

As a foreign national it was possible for her to gain access to Gaza, albeit with some difficulty, unlike her Palestinian or Israeli colleagues in Activestills. So she felt a strong sense of duty to continue working there. She covered the Israeli bombardment in 2012 and acknowledges that it has got harder witnessing the suffering in Gaza as the siege has gone on. Referring to the Israeli bombardment of 2014 she said:

> I was trying to have a break from working in Palestine but after what happened last summer was so horrendous, I felt the responsibility to go there. I keep going back to Gaza because there is so much to say about what happened and what is going on there.[29]

A major recent project tackles the suffering taking place there with enormous respect and compassion. The *Obliterated Families* multimedia web documentary, made in collaboration with journalist Ala Qandil, documents the experience of fifty-three families who lost many of their kin in the bombardment of Gaza in 2014.[30] She is highly aware of the difficulties of asking people to talk about their experiences. In one part of the work, she describes meeting Hussein al-Najjar, who had lost twenty-two members of his family. She offered him a photograph that she had taken on the day of his family's funeral. He refused to take it, saying that he did not want remember that day. She suddenly felt ashamed of her insensitivity:

> I felt that for a moment I had lost that delicate balance between documenting the tragedy and bringing more sorrow

into the already devastated lives of the survivors ... Everyone wants an original account of the attack, a piece of their intimate feelings, a few personal details ...

But as Rajah Shehadeh points out in his foreword to *Obliterated Families*:

> The authors of this documentary are not among those who try to take anything. Instead, they generously give back to the people of Gaza.[31]

Another example of her response to the 2014 bombardment of Gaza was her powerful series of portraits, *This Used to be My Bedroom*, which showed children in their destroyed bedrooms, in the remains of what had been their own private universe. Anne asked each child, 'What do you miss the most from your room?' The images and words convey a palpable sense of their shock and loss. For example, Yarra Ziada, aged nine years, from Shuja'iyya, said that she missed her games and red dress and was afraid that the bombings would start again.[32]

Documentary photographers sometimes share their work with the communities or individuals that they photograph in acknowledgement of the bond between photographer and subject. In the case of Ann Paq and Activestills, this has been a central aspect to their practice from the outset. The agency grew out of an informal group of three photography students and one Argentinian, and as far back as 2005 they were displaying informal exhibitions of their images on the streets.[33] This was a new approach to exhibiting work, facilitated by the availability of inexpensive digital prints. Utilising digital technology in order to democratise access to photography and the distribution of images has always been a key aspect of their work. Their strategy as a group of photographers is to back Palestinian social justice campaigns by donating their images to the campaigns that they have photographed.[34] They also make a practice of standing with the demonstrators rather than the police or the army, often spending a great deal of time at an event because they do not have the same deadline pressures as news photographers. Activestills' work supports a political and historical narrative of Palestinian resistance. Their images of demonstrations have been printed in large format and carried on subsequent demonstrations by protestors. As the writer Dina Matar puts it in another context, Palestinians can thus be seen as, '*actors* at the centre of critical phases of their modern history'.[35]

There is an urgent need to constantly update such a narrative of resistance, not least because in the West Bank and Gaza, freedom of the press is far from guaranteed. The authorities frequently attempt to censor the news by physical intimidation and the arrest of members of the media. According to the Committee to Protect Journalists, which monitors the safety of journalists around the world, between 2000 and 2014, sixteen journalists died in the West Bank and Gaza; all but one of them at the hands of the Israeli forces.[36] In 2014, during the Israeli bombardment of Gaza, seventeen journalists died. The vast majority of media workers who have died as a result of Israeli fire were specifically targeted, despite the fact that their status as members of the media was clearly evident; they were wearing clothing marked 'press' or were in a building that housed media organisations, like the Basha Tower in Gaza. During their previous 2012 assault on Gaza, the Israeli government admitted that they targeted journalists, claiming they were acting as human shields for Hamas.[37] By comparison, only one journalist died during the Troubles in Northern Ireland between 1969 and 2001.[38]

The Israeli forces often target members of the Palestinian media and it makes little difference whether they are working for a local or an international news organisation. In 2011 Abed Qusini, while working for Reuters, was targeted by an Israeli soldier, who fired a stun grenade at his head. As a result, he suffered nerve damage to his neck and lost 30 per cent of his hearing. He was also left with permanent tinnitus. Abed survived but in 2003, his friend and fellow photojournalist Nazih Darwazeh was not as lucky. He was shot and killed by the Israeli military, as he stood next to him. They were both covering the situation in Nablus after the IDF had entered the city centre in tanks. Abed describes his working life:

> So you are in war. It is risky to your life. During the last years I [was] injured many times and this made it difficult for me and for the family ... The worst thing is that there is no guarantee on your life.[39]

Despite this, Abed feels lucky to work for a caring employer unlike many of his colleagues:

> I know I'm lucky to work with an international agency but there are many many locals who don't even have that

guarantee. I have health insurance for me and my kids, [and] life insurance for the future.

The Israeli army constantly targets young Palestinian photographers, many of whom are very vulnerable because they are working without formal press accreditation. Haim Schwarczenberg published a video in February 2016 on YouTube showing how a Palestinian journalist was singled out for arrest in Hebron when he was standing with other press photographers:

> [This] incident … is highly typical of the way the Israeli army treats journalists, especially the Palestinian ones: soldiers disrupt the journalists' work in the field, as the latter attempt to document military violence. Then the local commander declares the area a 'closed military zone' and arrests a Palestinian journalist for merely being there.

Anne Paq sees many Palestinians taking up cameras to document what is going on in their communities and she too is angry about how they are targeted by the Israeli forces:

> I have witnessed a lot of young Palestinian photographers and video camera men being arrested or their cameras broken. Some of them have spent quite some time in prison just because they were documenting what was going on. Yes, some international photographers or activists have been injured or arrested at different times and the worst thing that can happen to them is deportation. But as a young Palestinian it's a different story.

Palestinian photographers also find it very difficult to acquire expensive protective clothing; the bullet-proof vests, helmets or gas masks, which are supplied to staffers. For example, Samar Abu Elouf in Gaza has been a photographer since 2010. She finally acquired some protective gear in 2017. During the bombardment in 2014 she had no such equipment and she took enormous risks whilst covering the effects of the Israeli destruction in Gaza City. Half-seriously and half-ironically, she wore a domestic cooking pot on her head as a makeshift hard-hat, along with a home-made tabard with the word 'press' written on it, in place of a bullet-proof vest. She encountered mockery from some young men, who asked her what was for dinner. Determined to work, when she could not afford taxis she hitched rides to the Gaza border, in order to photograph the Israeli tanks massed there.

> During the war [in 2014] I went long distances and I had to get into cars whose drivers I don't know. It's very dangerous, and you are not protected, you're not recognised by anyone, you're not [considered] a journalist.[40]

While she was documenting the devastation in the Shuja'iyya district in 2014, survivors who were in a state of shock after the destruction of their homes smashed her camera.[41] She had to beg them to let her have the memory card and it took her a month to get her equipment repaired. During that time she borrowed no less than nine cameras in order to keep working. She found the temporary loss 'very tough'. She explains, 'Losing the camera was like losing your spirit, [as] if someone took out your soul.'

DEFENDING HOPE

She was deeply frustrated because she longed to photograph everything that was going on:

> There were bombings near my house. It was awful that I did not have my camera to go out and to photograph this immediately.

She has what Palestinians characterise as the Gazan spirit of energy and ingenuity. Like the young artists in Anne Paq's short film on Gaza, *Not a Dreamland*, a passion for her work keeps her going. For Samar, photography is about stopping a moment of time that can never be repeated. She derives enormous satisfaction and pleasure from seeing her reportage work published. But living in Gaza means that she is cut off from networks, from stories she would like to cover, and from potential employers. So she uses social media, and sometimes publications pick up her work. During the 2014 bombardment she was published locally and internationally.[42] *The New York* magazine ran a spread of her images, which included one of a newborn baby saved from her dead mother's womb after the latter was hit by an Israeli airstrike, and another of a man holding the charred and severed hand of someone killed during an Israeli airstrike on a tower block in Gaza. Living through seven weeks of bombardments in 2014, without any possibility of escape, left its mark and Samar has suffered from post-traumatic stress disorder (PTSD).

However, she is passionate about telling the 'humanitarian story' of life in Gaza and is building a professional reputation, despite facing huge obstacles as a woman photographer (see fig. 5). She derives occasional satisfaction from the fact that society like Gaza, some stories are available to her that it would not be possible for a man to cover. Samar has four school-age children and her husband is a taxi driver, so money for equipment is not plentiful. She contends with the disapproval of her extended family. Fortunately, she has the support of her husband and she has been winning prizes and recognition for her work. The International Committee of the Red Cross published a series of her portraits of Gazan women to mark International Women's Day in 2016.[43] In May that year she was also one of twelve participants in the Visual Storytelling Photography Workshop in Gaza run by the World Press Photo Foundation.[44] She would like to travel but as a resident of Gaza, this is extremely difficult. Long delays at the Rafah border crossing stopped her from attending a photography awards ceremony in the United Arab Emirates in 2016. Yet she says that, 'I find myself only with the camera. The camera is the inspiration giving my soul warmth and safety.'

In the last ten years, digital images, distributed via the internet, have become an important tool often used by citizen-journalists or participants at demonstrations, who, finding themselves under attack, turn to their mobile phone cameras to record the events taking place, in order to publicise the events in a national and global context. Narmin Abu Haya, who lives in Hebron, was at the Al-Aqsa Mosque in Jerusalem in late 2012 when she and others came under attack from the Israeli police who used stun grenades and tear gas to disperse Palestinians who wanted to pray at the mosque. Despite finding herself suddenly in the midst of a melee of panicking people she started filming on her smartphone. Her courage was remarkable:

DEFENDING **HOPE**

> I had the [tear gas] bombs between my legs, [there was] shooting and shouting ... but I insisted to keep filming. Hearing is different from seeing things – I wanted to show the world what is going on.[45]

Narmin is now a volunteer on the B'Tselem Camera Project. It was set up in 2007 as a way of countering the Israeli dominated news narrative about life in Palestine by creating a network of Palestinian videographers who would record life on the ground. There was a great deal of concern at the lack of visual testimony recording the Palestinian perspective. The Israeli-based human rights organisation B'Tselem, understood the importance of collecting and publishing video evidence of human rights violations. So they distributed small video cameras to Palestinians and gave them training on how to film their everyday lives, especially the harassment and attacks from Jewish settlers, the Israeli Defence Forces or the Israeli Border Police. B'Tselem have produced films including one showing a Palestinian perspective on life inside Gaza, and another film documenting life in Hebron. For example, the al-Haddah family shot the film *Smile and the World will Smile Back* about their experience of constant house searches.[46]

B'Tselem is very aware of the risks that its video volunteers can face when documenting life under military rule. So they provide legal assistance to all their volunteers whenever necessary, as well as regular training. As the video department director Ehab Tarabieh explained, they also provide each of them with a signed letter from the IDF Central Command saying 'that anyone is allowed to film as long as it does not pose a danger to the security forces or interfere with their activity'.[47]

This Life Goes Out to the World Through Our Lenses

This offers limited protection. B'Tselem has field researchers who act as liaison between the videographers and their office in Jerusalem, and who are involved in training and supporting volunteers. Musa Abu Hashhash runs the office in Hebron with Manal al-Ja'bri. They are proud of the contribution that the fifty Hebron volunteers make to a project that has two hundred volunteers spread over the occupied territories. He says:

> Hebron never stops supplying videos. The volunteers here, especially the women, are very enthusiastic. The video project is still the most important project in B'Tselem, especially since we stopped the legal cooperation with the Israelis.[48]

The Camera Project does more than record events; it also empowers participants and gives them hope that they can mitigate the effects of the Israeli occupation. In 2013, not long after her experience of being under attack at Al-Aqsa Mosque, Narmin started to volunteer with B'Tselem's innovative project. Having a video camera on hand to film attacks by Jewish settlers has provided her family with some protection. She explains:

> In the beginning my hands shook and the pictures were shaky. Soon I became stronger, more aware of what I was doing. We were afraid of the settlers at the beginning but now when we hold the camera they stop attacking. So we are protecting ourselves with the camera.

Standing on Narmin's roof, it is clear that they live, as she says, 'In between [Jewish] settlers from all directions.' Hostile neighbours surround her home on three sides. The rest of her family have now got involved, including her husband Mahmoud and all her children. According to B'Tselem, the involvement of other members of a volunteer's family is quite common, especially when the family is living in such difficult circumstances and has become the target of harassment from the Israeli security forces and their Jewish settler neighbours.[49] They have received a great deal of unwanted attention from the Israeli army. For example, over a six-day period in April 2015, the IDF came to their home daily, by day and by night, to carry out searches and identity checks in what B'Tselem describes as a 'saga of harassment'. Narmin and her family responded by recording the constant visits from the military on video.[50] One day in May 2015, a group of approximately forty soldiers took over her roof en masse. They stayed for about an hour and photographed themselves and the family.[51] Narmin describes the aims of her video work:

> In general to liberate our country, but particularly I have to show the rest of the world what is happening to us so they can help us in liberating our mosques, [and] opening Shuhada Street … This is what I hope.

Since 2001, Shuhada Street, the main shopping thoroughfare in the centre of Hebron, has been closed to Palestinians. The old city centre is now deserted. Hundreds of Palestinians currently have to climb over roofs and walls in order to find back routes into their homes, because they are forbidden by military edict from walking down the street. The once thriving commercial centre of Hebron is now a ghost town. Residents cannot move around freely and

Fig. 13: The wall, near Bethlehem.
Photo: Joanne O'Brien

Fig. 14: Palestinian workers queuing before dawn in July 2007 at a checkpoint near Bethlehem in the West Bank. Many thousands do this daily in order to travel to work in Israeli and Palestinian cities beyond the Green Line. Photo: Anne Paq/Activestills

Fig. 15: Mustafa Tamimi being shot fatally in the head at close range with a tear-gas canister by an Israeli soldier in Nabi Saleh, 2011. Villagers had been protesting against the confiscation of village land by settlers. Photo: Haim Schwarczenberg

Fig. 16: Narmin Abu Haya, a volunteer on B'Tselem's Camera Project in Hebron. Photo: Joanne O'Brien

Fig. 19: An Israeli watchtower near Shuyukh al-Arrub in the West Bank.
Photo: Joanne O'Brien

Fig. 17: Suzan Fawaz Zaraqu, another volunteer on B'Tselem's Camera Project in Hebron. Photo: Joanne O'Brien

Fig. 18: Battir, outside of Bethlehem in the West Bank. A herdsman with his goats near the Hijaz railway line between Tel Aviv and Jerusalem which Palestinians are not permitted to use. Photo: Joanne O'Brien

Fig. 21: Rabbi Arik Ascherman, Torat Tzedek, during a visit to a Bedouin village in the South Mount Hebron area, 2013. He has been deeply involved in attempts to protect Palestinian farmers from attacks and land confiscations by settlers.
Photo: Joanne O'Brien

Fig. 19: An Israeli watchtower near Shuyukh al-Arrub in the West Bank.
Photo: Joanne O'Brien

Fig. 20: Khaled Mnasrh farms in the West Bank village of Wadi Foukin. He is short of water because of the settlement of Battir Illit behind him. He suffers from attacks by the settlers and damage to his land from the sewage released on to it.
Photo: Joanne O'Brien

Fig. 21: Rabbi Arik Ascherman, Torat Tzedek, during a visit to a Bedouin village in the South Mount Hebron area, 2013. He has been deeply involved in attempts to protect Palestinian farmers from attacks and land confiscations by settlers.
Photo: Joanne O'Brien

Fig. 22: Raji Sourani, founder and director of the Palestinian Centre for Human Rights, standing at the destroyed Italian Plaza in Gaza City.
Photo: Joanne O'Brien

Fig. 23: Palestinian woman Mahfouza Ishtayeh (65) embraces the trunk of her olive tree after it was destroyed by settlers in the West Bank village of Salem, near Nablus, 27 November 2005. Photo: Abed Qusini

Fig. 23: Palestinian woman Mahfouza Ishtayeh (65) embraces the trunk of her olive tree after it was destroyed by settlers in the West Bank village of Salem, near Nablus, 27 November 2005. Photo: Abed Qusini

This Life Goes Out to the World Through Our Lenses

often find streets blocked by army checkpoints. B'Tselem field researchers Manal al-Ja'bri and Musa Abu Hashhash try to record such incidents. In June 2017 whilst they were doing so, Israeli Border Police arrested them both.[52]

B'Tselem does not specifically send the volunteers on journalistic missions but instead encourages them to operate autonomously and film what they see around them, and to see themselves as citizen-journalists. Safety is a paramount concern. Ehab Tarabieh, director of the Camera Project says:

> In each meeting with the volunteers we emphasise that their safety is [most] important thing above all. We never send [them] on missions to cover incidents, we ask them to document their daily life at their homes, their neighbourhoods and their lands.

Using a video camera can sometimes act as a defence for Palestinians who have to endure constant attention from the Israeli army or the indignity of being woken in the small hours by an army patrol demanding to search their home and scrutinise their identification papers. As Yoav Gross, former video department director of the Camera Project says:

> The camera has become something that is no longer in the exclusive realm of the artist … it is used as a tool by so many people.

It can take some courage to get out a camera and start filming. But Yoav is convinced that 'most of the times, it helps rather than puts you in danger'. However, when a volunteer captures a particularly controversial event they can face a lot of intimidation and pressure. This happened in March 2016 to Imad Abu Shamsyia when he filmed the extra-judicial killing of a Palestinian by a soldier in Hebron.[53] Ehab Tarabieh explains that almost a year later he is still living under a great deal of strain:

> Since he documented the extrajudicial killing in Hebron in March 2016, settlers keep harassing and threatening him … and the soldiers and the police don't even try to protect him and his family. Imad and Fayza his wife … they are still filming, it's not easy, they are human rights activists who live under heavy circumstances. If they stop fighting for their rights, they will lose their home as [have] many others from the old city of Hebron.

However, another volunteer in Hebron, Sozan Fawaz Zaraqu (who is also a professional wedding videographer) says that the most satisfying aspect of the work she does is:

> Protecting my neighbours. I cannot stop the army violence. If I tried, I would be a victim [myself]. I have gone to the street and tried to shout, to do something to help … but it did not work. So I thought of another choice, which is more effective … once the camera is facing the soldiers and the settlers, they start thinking there will be evidence against them. The most interesting thing [is seeing] the soldiers coming to attack, very enthusiastic, and when they see a camera, they stop. It makes me feel very happy, I feel strong.[54]

This Life Goes Out to the World Through Our Lenses

In May 2016, Sozan filmed Israeli soldiers near a flashpoint between Jewish settlers and Palestinian residents on the road leading to the Tomb of the Patriarch. The soldiers put some Palestinian children up against a wall, then questioned and photographed them. Her video enabled B'Tselem to publicise the nature of life under military occupation and the actions of the IDF, who regularly intimidate minors.[55] Both Sozan and Narmin feel empowered by publicising their situation via their videos, which are published by B'Tselem on the internet. Musa Abu Hashhash says that: 'The volunteers are very happy when their videos are shown, sometimes by tens of thousands of people.' Sardonically, he adds, 'The army and the settlers make Hebron a special place.'

Like the B'Tselem volunteers and field researchers, news photographer Abed Qusini shares a sense of how imperative it is to tell the story of his community. However, he laments the fact that he 'cannot photograph normal life' and is often covering scenes of violent confrontation or suffering. He is based in Nablus where he has been working for Reuters since 1998. Before that he worked with the Associated Press (AP) as a cameraman. During the first intifada, when his children were very young, he went to some lengths to shield them from the terrible scenes that he filmed.[56] When he used to get home from work, he often had to edit what he had shot that day. But his children would crowd around him and want to sit on his knee, which put him in a quandary. 'I wanted [them] to do that but the pictures were awful.' So he often did the editing on his laptop out in the car and filing his pictures with AP before coming into the house. He felt strongly that it was his duty as a parent to protect the innocence and hope of his children:

DEFENDING **HOPE**

> I would try [to ensure] that there must be a hope that my kids [can] live normally. I wished for that, worked for that. Children, they are the hope of the future. I care about my children. They are the secret of life.

In common with Anne Paq and Samar Abu Elouf, he has a strong belief in the power of the single image: 'One shot is a story' (see fig. 23). He is also highly aware that as a local he often has a greater understanding and concern for events that are taking place. In contrast to his colleagues from abroad, he has the patience to wait for a story to unfold: 'A foreign journalist, they will leave [but] I'll think that there will be a picture in two hours' [time], so it's worth waiting.' He feels that is it important the Palestinian perspective gets through and is optimistic about the power of photographs to alert the world to his people's suffering. He has a huge archive of images, which date back to the emergence of digital photography around 2003:

> I have a big archive. I am proud of what I do. I did a good history for Palestinians. Sometimes it's painful, sometimes it is good, and sometimes there is happiness or tears. We are writing Palestinian history in this way. And this life goes out to the world through our lenses.

Abed has a strong sense of his duty to tell the story and wants to see more Palestinians 'shooting pictures and writing':

> We are living here and part of a nation, which struggles for freedom and dignity in life. So why surrender and go back

home? If you will not do it, nobody in the world will see. Pictures are very important.

As anyone who knows photographers will tell you, they are generally individualists. Yet all the photographers discussed here share a collective hope that their work will contribute to the ending of the Israeli occupation, or in the short term, counter the view of the Israeli government that all is well in the land. Each of them puts their own stamp on their work, whilst believing that photography and video can make a difference and help end the abuse of Palestinian human rights by Israel. They tackle their work with courage, ingenuity, thoughtfulness, and humanity. To borrow a phrase from Robert Hariman, they turn, 'an ethical lens' onto what they see.[57] They all urgently demand that we engage, that we keep looking and acknowledging the grave realities their work reveals. Their work is a contemporary and historical portrait of the social and human consequences of the Israeli occupation and colonisation. But it also portrays a record of their own personal interactions with the people in front of their cameras; this is photography as a record of encounters. It is the spirit of these encounters and the expectation of a morally engaged audience, which offers hope.

DEFENDING HOPE

Notes:
1. Anne Paq, interview with the author, 26 January 2015.
2. 'As long as there are cameras in this world, photographs will continue to be made simultaneously by different people and heterogeneous realities will be presented that will eat away at any supposed monopoly.' Ariella Azoulay, *The Civil Contract of Photography*, New York: Zone Books, 2008, p. 190.
3. The occupied Palestinian territories (OPT) in the West Bank are divided into three zones and Israelis are forbidden from entering Zones A and B and most cities and towns in Area C.
4. Azoulay, *Civil Contract*, p. 194. See also chapter six 'Photographing the Verge of Catastrophe', pp. 289–373.
5. For example: Filmmakers: Emad Burnat, *5 Broken Cameras*; Fida Qishta, *Where Should the Birds Fly*; Dani Rosenberg and Yoav Gross, *Susya*; Photographers: Haitham Khatib from Bil'in, *Occupied Palestine: Through My Lens* (Palestine in Print, 2015), and the rest of the Activestills collective.
6. For the purposes of brevity, hereafter, I shall refer to them all as photographers.
7. Interview with the author, London, 24 June 2015.
8. According to Breaking the Silence, the ex-IDF combatants' organisation, 'A significant portion of the IDF's offensive actions are not intended to prevent a specific act of terrorism, but rather to punish, deter, or tighten control over the Palestinian population.' p. 26. www.breakingthesilence.org.il/wp-content/uploads/2011/02/Occupation_of_the_Territories_Eng.pdf.
9. Robert Hariman, 'Watching War Evolve' in *The Violence of the Image: Photography and International Conflict*, Liam Kennedy and Caitlin Patrick (eds), London: I.B. Tauris, 2014, pp. 139–63. Inequality and social deprivation is also a condition for Arabs who are citizens of Israel as John McCarthy eloquently documents in *You Can't Hide the Sun: A Journey Through Israel and Palestine*, London: Transworld Publishers, 2012.
10. Nidal al-Mughrabi, 'Energy crisis leaves Gaza with barely four hours of power a day', Reuters, 12 January 2017. www.reuters.com/article/us-palestinians-gaza-energy/energy-crisis-leaves-gaza-with-barely-four-hours-of-power-a-day-idUSKBN14W1YG/.
11. Interview with the author, Gaza, 9 February 2016.
12. For example, on 19 March 2017, in Hebron, more than fifteen soldiers seized eight-year-old Sufian Abu Hitah, who was out on the street barefoot, looking for a toy he had lost. He was held for more than an hour and taken to several homes in an attempt to force him to identify children who had thrown stones and a Molotov cocktail at the Kiryat Arba settlement. Eventually, several women managed to extricate him and return him to his mother. www.btselem.org/video/20170326_soldiers_drag_child_from_house_to_house/. Another frequent subject covered by B'tselem videographers is Palestinian farmers being attacked by Jewish settlers who are attempting to put them off their land.
13. Report on the Jordan Valley, 'The ban on Palestinian construction and development in the Jordan Valley takes a particularly harsh toll on the roughly ten thousand residents of more than fifty Palestinian communities in Area C that Israel is attempting by various means to drive from their homes and land.' www.btselem.org/jordan_valley. Updated 6 October 2013.
14. The town of Modi'in Illit is known by the Palestinians as *Kiryat Sefer* (Book Town) and was built on expropriated Palestinian land.
15. The settlers frequently enjoy virtual legal impunity as they destroy Palestinian crops and property with the collusion of the Israeli state forces. An ex-IDF soldier testified

This Life Goes Out to the World Through Our Lenses

to Breaking the Silence, 'As far as we're concerned, we're in a situation in which we're in territory where the settlers are always right. As a soldier, if you have to choose between a settler and a Palestinian, or between a settler and a left-wing activist – you choose the settler, no matter the situation.' www.breakingthesilence.org.il/testimonies/database/733128.

16. Bassem Abu Rahma was hit by a tear gas canister and his death was captured in Emad Burnat's the Oscar-nominated documentary *5 Broken Cameras*. He was a popular and much-loved figure in the local community and there is an iconic image of him running whilst flying a kite, taken by Oren Ziv of Activestills.
17. Hamde Abu Rahma, *Roots Run Deep*, Hamdeaburahma.com, 2013.
18. Interview with the author, Bil'in, 10 February 2016.
19. Nabi Saleh is a village of six hundred people who have mounted weekly protests against the expropriation of their land by the nearby Jewish settlement of Halamish since 2010. The village has been a beacon for the non-violent Palestinian protest movement against the occupation. Their protests were met by excessive violence, two people have died (Mustafa and Rushdi Tamimi), and over the years approximately three hundred and fifty protestors have been injured. In 2016, the villagers suspended their weekly protests because of the high numbers of injuries and the constant use of tear gas and skunk by the IDF in their small village.
20. Breaking the Silence was founded in 2004 by a group of Israeli army veterans who had served in Hebron. They collect testimonies from soldiers and document the abuses carried out the IDF against Palestinian civilians living under military occupation. They aim to raise awareness amongst Israelis about what is being done in their name and also to highlight its effects on Israeli conscripts. They oppose the military occupation. www.breakingthesilence.org.il/about/organisation/
21. www.schwarczenberg.com/. He also has nearly nine thousand followers on Facebook, see www.facebook.com/schwarczenberg/.
22. Interview with the author, Tel Aviv, 12 December 2017.
23. www.schwarczenberg.com/. He also has nearly nine thousand followers on Facebook, see www.facebook.com/schwarczenberg/.
24. Haim also spoke about the death of Mustafa Tamimi to an Amnesty International Israel conference in Tel Aviv on 31 January 2014, entitled 'The Use of Excessive Force in Suppression of Civil Protest'. Mustafa's cousin, Rushdi Tamimi, was shot dead by the IDF in 2012.
25. www.youtube.com/watch?v=QRHqU8H1CVk/
26. Interview with the author, London, 13 December 2014.
27. Interview with the author, London, 26 January 2015.
28. The short film was produced by Anne Paq and Activestills. www.electronicintifada.net/content/video-images-and-sounds-gazas-vibrant-subculture-not-dreamland/11825/. This was not her first foray into video. In 2007, she co-directed her first video short in 2007, *Bethlehem Checkpoint, 4AM*. The following year she worked on a video short in with residents of Gaza's Shu'fat camp, called *Intensive Care Unit*, based on a poem by Mahmoud Darwish produced by Voices Beyond Walls. www.voicesbeyondwalls.org/index.html/
29. Interview with the author, London, 26 January 2015.
30. *Obliterated Families: The Stories of Families Whose Lives were Shattered During the 2014 Israeli Offensive on the Gaza Strip* by Anne Paq and Ala Qandil (2017). The project looks at fifty-three families. Ten families alone lost ninety members between them. www.obliteratedfamilies.com/en/about/; accessed 21 September 2017. For an example of a similar work of remembrance in another medium, see *Drawing the Kafr Qasem Massacre* by Samia Halaby, Amsterdam: Schilt, 2017.

31. Rajah Shehadeh, Foreword, www.obliteratedfamilies.com/en/rajah-shehadeh/
32. She points out that children as young as six years old have already experienced three military offensives. www.aljazeera.com/indepth/inpictures/2014/11/pictures-i-miss-my-games-red-dr-201411693347431796.html. In 2015, Anne Paq did a touring exhibition in the Netherlands called *Gaza Inside Out*.
33. Oren Ziv, Yotam Ronen and Keren Manor met on a photography course in Israel and started working together informally, covering demonstrations against the Israeli separation wall in 2005.
34. They also support other social justice campaigns such as the LGBTQ movement, the rights of women, migrants and asylum seekers and housing rights. See *Activestills, Photography as Protest in Palestine/Israel*, Vered Maimon and Shiraz Grinbaum (eds), London: Pluto, 2016.
35. Dina Matar, *What it Means to be Palestinian: Stories of Palestinian Peoplehood*, London & New York: I.B. Taurus, 2011. An important aspect of Activestills work is the 'performativity', see Vered Maimon 'Surviving Images and Images of Survival: On Activestills' Photographs of Protest', in *Activestills Photography as Protest in Palestine/Israel*, Vered Maimon and Shiraz Grinbaum (eds), London: Pluto, 2016, pp. 182–93.
36. Four media support workers have also died in the same period, two of them in Gaza. The Committee to Protect Journalists reported that Suleiman Abdul-Rahim al-Ashi, who was working for the Hamas-affiliated newspaper, *Palestine*, was killed with his colleague and support worker Mohammad Matar Abdo, by Fatah gunmen in Gaza on 13 May 2007. The other three media support workers died as a result of Israeli fire. www.cpj.org/killed/mideast/israel-and-the-occupied-palestinian-territory/; accessed 8 September 2017.
37. www.electronicintifada.net/blogs/charlotte-silver/israeli-spokesperson-admits-targeting-journalists-gaza/
38. The relationship between the press, the British army, and the paramilitaries remained contentious and news coverage was frequently subjected to censorship. However, it is striking that Martin O'Hagan of *The Sunday World* was the only journalist murdered during the Troubles. He died at the hands of Loyalist paramilitaries in September 2001, after he had been investigating the activities of Loyalist gangsters. www.pressgazette.co.uk/uk-journalists-who-lost-their-lives-covering-conflict-2000/.
39. 'Hebron: Israeli soldiers target and arrest Palestinian journalist, 25 February 2016.' www.youtube.com/watch?v=jsVxWsGJvqY/
40. Interview with the author, Gaza, 9 February 2016.
41. An eastern district of Gaza city, where one hundred and fifty thousand people lost their homes during the Israeli bombardment in 2015.
42. Katie Zavadski, 'The Photo of a Newborn Baby Is One of the Most Heartbreaking and Disturbing Images to Come Out the Gaza War'. nymag.com/daily/intelligencer/2014/07/heartbreaking-image-of-a-newborn-in-gaza.html.
43. Portraits of women of Gaza, Samar Abu Elouf, 13 March 2016. www.blogs.icrc.org/ilot/2016/03/13/portraits-of-women-of-gaza/.
44. 'Announcing the participants of Visual Storytelling Photography Workshop Gaza', *World Press Photo*, 15 April 2016. www.worldpressphoto.org/news/2016-04-15/announcing-participants-visual-storytelling-photography-workshop-gaza/.
45. Interview with the author, Hebron, 11 February 2016.
46. *Smile and the World Will Smile Back*, by the al-Haddad family, Ehab Tarabieh and Yoav Gross, (B'Tselem, 2014). www.btselem.org/btselem/smile/en/; *Gaza – An Inside Look* (2009), a series of short films by young people, e.g. www.btselem.org/

This Life Goes Out to the World Through Our Lenses

video/2009/10/gaza-inside-look-hip-hop-lesson/; *My Own Private Gaza*, a video blog by Khaled al-'Azayzeh that was launched in 2012. www.btselem.org/videochannel/gaza-blog/; *The Boy from H2* (2017) dir. by Helen Yanovsky. www.btselem.org/press_releases/20170109_the_boy_from_h2/.

47. Interview by email, 20 February 2017. In 2016, B'Tselem stopped supplying its video evidence of human rights infringements and illegal activities by the army and the police to the Israeli authorities. They decided that they could no longer collude with what they saw as the Israeli authorities' pretence of investigating human rights abuses.
48. Interview with the author, 6 September 2017.
49. Hebron is an especially tense place. The city is divided into two parts: H1, which is Arab (population approximately two hundred thousand), and H2, the old city, which is home to some thirty-five thousand Palestinians and between five hundred–eight hundred and fifty Jewish settlers who are protected by the Israeli army whilst the settlers generally treat the Arab population with racist contempt and violence.
50. See report by B'Tselem, www.btselem.org/hebron/20150525_harassment_of_abu_haya_family/. Soldiers try to keep members of Abu Haya family from filming them searching their home, 2015. www.btselem.org/video/20150526_harassment_of_abu_haya_family/.
51. www.btselem.org/video/20150526_harassment_of_abu_haya_family_soldiers_on_roof/.
52. They were both later released.
53. Abu Shamsysia filmed the killing of 'Abd al-Fatah a-Sharif by Israeli soldier Elor Azaria in March 2016. The soldier was tried for manslaughter and given eighteen months, reduced to fourteen months on appeal. www.btselem.org/press_releases/20160901_btselem_volunteer_life_threatened/.
54. Author's interview with Sozan Fawaz Zaraqu, Hebron, February 2016.
55. Fourteen children under the age of fourteen years were detained and photographed. Some of them were as young as eight years old. www.btselem.org/hebron/20160602_soldiers_photograph_minors_in_hebron/.
56. The First Intifada took place between 1987–1993.
57. Robert Hariman 'Watching War Evolve' in *The Violence of the Image: Photography and International Conflict*, Liam Kennedy and Caitlin Patrick (eds), London: I.B. Tauris, 2014, pp. 139–63.

High Hopes

Angela Godfrey-Goldstein

'WE DON'T HAVE THE LUXURY OF DESPAIR.' – *The late Maha abu Dayyeh, founder/director of The Women's Centre for Legal Aid & Counselling (WCLAC)*

'HOPE IS DEFINITELY NOT THE SAME THING AS OPTIMISM. IT IS NOT THE CONVICTION THAT SOMETHING WILL TURN OUT WELL, BUT THE CERTAINTY THAT SOMETHING MAKES SENSE REGARDLESS OF HOW IT TURNS OUT.' – *Václav Havel*

Lobbying a diplomat at the UN in New York recently, someone whom I had known years earlier when he served in Palestine, I detected a certain cynicism, even a patronising tone beneath the familiar friendship. 'Angela! You're still going! Amazing!!' I sensed that he thought I hadn't yet realised the futility of obstinate persistence, or simply hadn't the intelligence to understand what he and others had long since concluded: that the situation in Palestine is hopeless, a waste of time, an insoluble problem. Better to move on and leave it.

How far from the truth! Hope is a question of free choice and willpower rather than a response to external reality. But, after thirty-seven years, development of that spirit remains a challenge. It is an internal, spiritual struggle or, some would say, *jihad*. Some may ask whether, when Hope left Pandora's Box last:

was Hope the final vice or the redeeming virtue? Either definition undervalues hope in my view. Hope is one of the most efficient tinders to spark the human spirit, together with free choice, freedom and a strong sense of humour. But, like the quest for peace, it is not for the faint-hearted, the weak or the pale of spirit.

I came to Israel thirty-seven years ago, inspired by an unusually gifted teacher whom I met in South Africa a few years previously. One of the lessons I learned from him over ten years in Israel-Palestine was the vital importance of hope and positive energy. Without hope, the human spirit crumbles, we turn inwards in despair and let creativity stagnate; or as Terje Larsen says, in the archive footage we used in a short film I produced (*High Hopes*) about Bedouin displacement: 'When hope disappears, then politics collapses.'

Choices, which we make every moment, consciously or unconsciously, are always before us. The stronger the spirit, the better we can rise up and fight back, non-violently, with as much love as the ego will allow to flourish. It takes us towards what is useful, towards the light. If, as I believe, hope opens doors and keeps creativity alive – whereas pessimism or despair make us give up – why not choose hope? The answer makes all the difference between buying into failure, allowing the defeatism of others or a contrary political agenda to swamp one's spirits, or kick-starting the spirit that fights back, takes risks and carries on despite everything.

One of my arguments with the agenda of those in power in Israel is their short-sightedness in not recognising the sacred and oneness in all life, including the environment. They seem bent on separation, exclusivity and alienation.

High Hopes

A major influence has been Sinai, which I first visited in 1996. Sinai is often referred to as 'the heart chakra of the world'. So, this is a love story — a classic, even a great love story, about a land, a landscape and a people who live there. A story filled with romance and depths of silence: the silence that only the desert offers. And a story to be told and understood on many levels. A modern morality tale, taking place in a spiritual homeland. A story to be heard by those who can hear; words to be understood by those who can understand. And, of course, things to be seen only by those who see deeply.

From this you may sense, I hope, what the desert is about, why seekers and sages are so influenced by it, why explorers are in love with its silence, its pristine nature, its vast open wildness and its closeness to natural laws. Environmentalists and nature-lovers easily fall for its ancient energy and magic. In these days of modern development and so-called 'progress' there is a growing, and unmet, need to protect this natural heritage and all those exquisitely beautiful places. If we allow deserts such as Sinai to be turned into extensions of major cities such as Cairo (as just one example of a worldwide trend), is there a price to be paid? And if so, by whom? I think we all pay a high price.

In 1997 I travelled to Cairo and to Amman to ask government representatives and environmentalists for permission, as an Israeli, to work jointly with them in Sinai. The response was generous and open: 'Welcome. We need people like you in Sinai.'

So, just two years after my first visit, with Friends of the Earth Middle East, we planned a three-year ecotourism project that I was to manage. Our vision was for Egyptian, Jordanian and

DEFENDING HOPE

Israeli NGOs to work together to solve environmental problems in Sinai, especially those caused by tourism development – sustainable use of water, recycling, safeguarding the underwater coral reefs and more.

However, the project had to be abandoned, soon after the funds were secured, because of the unravelling of the Oslo Accords and the strain in official relationships between Egypt and Israel. Forces beyond my control had intervened to end the cooperative work – should one give up?

Gently encouraged by Bedouin friends living there to move to Sinai, hope returned as I found myself organising divers to conduct underwater clean-ups in Sinai with a team that involved Israeli marine biologists, Egyptian National Parks rangers, Jordanian divers from the Royal Diving Centre, international instructors from Dahab and Sharm el Sheikh and local Bedouin. It was the first diving clean-up to transport the tons of garbage to a recycling plant, instead of hiding it in a *wadi* where it would inevitably return to the natural cycle of pollution. Next we battled to eliminate a Crown of Thorns plague attacking the soft corals of Ras Mohammed Marine Park, a $300-million-a-year diving industry. That work galvanised the local diving community to wrest control of the underwater environment from the Egyptian Ministry of Tourism, so that it is now professionally protected.

Other initiatives followed, working with NGOs in the north and south of Sinai for education, farming, women's empowerment, income generation and water production.

So, I had become a peace activist, simply by virtue of being perceived as an Israeli living in Sharm el Sheikh. Knowing basic Arabic and feeling comfortable in Arab culture after those years

High Hopes

in Egypt set me somewhat apart from my fellow Israelis, most of whom have never lived in the Arab world, or in neighbouring countries. An early challenge among the Bedouin was to overcome suspicions that I was with the Mossad. It was never easy. But even those challenges, once overcome, strengthened the spirit.

Without an education in matters of the spirit, I could never have penetrated as far as I have to the heart of Bedouin society, which is so loving, patient and human. I would not have had the privilege of knowing some of their wisest heads, sheikhs with brilliant minds, nor the ability to recognise some of the most insightful among them, who are the most simple. Our Western judgement criteria too often tend to miss the point.

Nothing spurs you on better than the kind of success which proves that one person can indeed change realities, in small or even large ways. I was walking around barefoot, sleeping in the desert alone with my dog, courting suspicion on all sides, but nevertheless on a mission that had success.

/ / /

Sinai is a magical landscape, especially those sacred spaces that are its majestic desert mountains. For Sinai's many followers it is an entire spiritual world that teaches freedom, healing, miracles, hope, love and *life* – spiritual aliveness and a beating heart. It is a world far from Israeli occupation, development goals, NGO business plans or missions of anthropology. A world where people look each other in the eyes openly, and hold the gaze naturally and fearlessly.

DEFENDING HOPE

My experience in Sinai after some twenty years gives me a huge appreciation for Bedouin culture – its environmental sustainability, its freedom and aliveness, its open and patient heart and its spirit. There is a specific Bedouin greeting I sometimes use that speaks directly to the spirit, which invariably produces a spirited, delighted response. Similarly, while many invoke *insha'allah* (God willing) with a doubting, tentative even begging inflection in their voice, I always make the point that *insha'allah* is a positive energy, much of which we can influence.

The second intifada broke out on 28 September 2000 on a Friday when I happened to be on a bus returning to Sinai from a doctor's appointment in Tel Aviv. I remember hearing on that bus radio of Prime Minister Ariel Sharon's deliberate provocation in ascending with a thousand Border Police to the Temple Mount in Jerusalem. This act alone immediately emptied Sinai of its Israeli tourists. The extended coastline of the Tarabin Bedouin region near Nuweiba became a ghost town. Then, a year later, on 11 September 2001, the situation imploded further with the attacks on New York. These developments left thousands of Bedouin in South Sinai with absolutely no income.

Living in the desert is tough. Bedouin life is tough. Survival in extreme conditions is tough. So, the Bedouin, perhaps more than most, appreciate the open heart that underlines the *modus vivendi* of their life. Whilst many have been corrupted by modernity, the occupation, the policies of divide and rule, and consumerism, something intrinsically Bedouin survives in that complex yet simple beating of a fighting heart, and the wisdom for life that comes from thousands of years of aliveness in desert. Think about this: a Bedouin can sleep anywhere. You and I need to find a bed, or a chair, or a roof over our heads, and probably grow slightly tense when it gets dark if we have no bed, chair or roof. Whereas Bedouin are comfortable in the 'nowness' of open nature, with far fewer anxieties or existential needs. And a greater, far greater appreciation of freedom, and need for it as a central principle of their life.

Meanwhile, the Bedouin inside Israel as citizens, or in the Occupied Palestinian Territory as refugees, no longer experience that freedom: they are the poorest of the poor, the most marginalised and – as herding pastoralists – the most endangered because they traditionally range over large areas of grazing land, which they have always owned. Shamefully, Israel has never allowed the Bedouin to register their land deeds, or recognised refugee Bedouins' right of return to their ancestral lands in the Negev (Naqab). On the contrary, Israelis regularly deny the Bedouin land ownership, deny their presence in Israel in 1948 and refer to them as 'nomads' when acknowledging their presence, in order to belittle the legitimacy of their presence on their land.

Ironically, after seventy years of trying to wipe out Bedouin culture, Israel has recently had to reverse a law banning black goats. It has become obvious that the forest fires now annually raging in Israel (due to increasing desertification from over-exploitation of the water table, drought and climate change and the poor choice in the 1940s of introducing non-endemic European pine trees to cover demolished Palestinian villages, while encouraging incoming refugees from Europe to feel at home with such familiar trees in their landscape) are less likely to be so catastrophic if goats are allowed to graze in those forests, to keep the undergrowth down.

DEFENDING HOPE

Human rights advocacy takes many forms, and cultural advocacy is a crucial way to reach people. Documentaries where people can see the reality for themselves are almost as powerful as tourists visiting the West Bank themselves.[1]

A decade ago, Israel developed the E-1 Plan, which envisages the mass population transfer of Palestinian Bedouin refugees from the periphery of Jerusalem to enable development of Ma'ale Adumim settlement: a policy defined by legal experts as a war crime.

In 2005, in response to peace activists' advocacy, the international community put sufficient pressure on Israel to freeze its three-thousand-acre E-1 settlement plan for three thousand five hundred units; it was told that this would represent 'the end of the Two State Solution' if it went ahead, due to its huge impact on Palestinian viability – road systems, open land reserves, splitting the West Bank in two and open access to Jerusalem and the 35 per cent of the Palestinian economy represented in the Ramallah/East Jerusalem/Bethlehem economic salient that would be denied.

Diplomatic pressure forced Israel to freeze it. Until now. Today, the development of E-1 is not only back on the agenda but has morphed into a far larger plan, which calls for the forced displacement of tens of thousands of refugee Bedouin and other Palestinian herders in Area C of the West Bank. There is also talk by Naftali Bennett, leader of a far-right party, The Jewish Home, of annexing the whole of Area C. Note that Area C is 60 per cent of the Occupied Palestinian Territory and represents the support system for Areas A and B – the remaining 40 per cent. Annexation would officially create an Israeli apartheid state stretching from the Jordan to the Mediterranean.

High Hopes

The scattered pastoral Bedouin were named 'gatekeepers of Jerusalem' by the late President Arafat. E-1 development, on land where the Bedouin now live, will utilise all remaining open land required for the natural expansion of Palestinian East Jerusalem. The only Palestinians, the Bedouin, will be removed from this region, 'Judaising' the open land stretching from East Jerusalem to Jericho by expanding Ma'ale Adumim onto that E-1 land, and making Greater Jerusalem demographically Jewish. Israel thus denies peace by foreclosing the creation of a viable Palestinian state, and continues policies of creeping annexation – illegal under international law.

The south and north access points to Jerusalem are already closed off by settlements, by the wall, by settler-only highways and by checkpoints. By closing off the last relatively open access to Jerusalem for Palestinian West Bankers, the E-1 plan denies Palestine free access to its economic heart, its religious sites, tourism industry, centre of social life, university campuses, or its specialist hospitals. This will be lost if wedges of settlements slice it up. Changed road systems will undermine the commercial viability of the Palestinian urban centres of Hebron and Ramallah. No wonder a leaked EU document of 2014 refers to E-1 development as a red line that may lead to EU sanctions against Israel. Carrot diplomacy exhausted, the EU now considers using the stick. But is still stuck at the stage of mere words – which settlers seem to read as 'green lights'.

The Nuweimeh Plan has also gone public, calling for forced displacement from the Jerusalem, Ramallah and Jericho governorates of some twelve thousand five hundred Bedouin herders to a purpose-built urban township on arid wasteland north of Jericho where they will be concentrated, forced to live against their will, at the loss of their traditional, rich, sustainable desert culture and pastoral economy. This is a grave breach of the Geneva Conventions, to which Israel is a signatory. Despite warnings that such policies of forcible displacement, if enacted, are war crimes – both Netanyahu and Lieberman have recently called for the 'relocation' of Bedouin, with Netanyahu stipulating in September 2017 that all West Bank Bedouin – some thirty thousand people – will be moved to the cities of Abu Dis and Jericho.

This is all reminiscent of how the US treated Native Americans in the nineteenth and early twentieth century. But that has since become the subject of landmark settlement deals, such as the Navajo's $554 million compensation: no equivalent settlement is planned for the Bedouin, just deeper and deeper displacement, and an end to their valuable and sustainable desert culture.

The implications for the Bedouin of forcible transfer into urban sites are catastrophic. They are likely, judging from previous botched attempts to move them, to sink into increasing poverty and unsustainability, dependent on handouts from the international community. Most indigenous Bedouin have already suffered under Israel's forced transfers, inside Israel, in the Negev, where Israel refuses to recognise Bedouin land title deeds, or accept their pastoralist presence.

Even without this planned displacement, the situation for the Bedouin is untenable in their current rural locations because they are denied planning permission. West Bank Bedouin are not allowed to build. They are also denied free access to education, as they are living in Area C, where the Israeli military provides them with neither schools nor transport, despite its obligations under international law as an occupying power. Over fifty Palestinian schools in Area C of the OPT have demolition orders threatening their existence. Where the Bedouin have built five schools, they are all the subject of high court litigation, often sponsored by extremist settler groups.

They are forbidden access to electricity, even if they live below high-tension electricity grids for the settlements or Palestinian West Bank towns. They have no vehicle access to settler-only road systems or to their Jerusalem market and holy sites. They suffer from gravely restricted access to health services, water, grazing lands or jobs, endure regular home demolitions and live in constant threat of settler violence. In one Bedouin community with whom I work, lands they bought in the 1970s are now unusable because of the pollution created by sewage flowing from nearby Israeli settlements. For over three years the Israeli authorities have failed to remedy the situation. In another Bedouin community near Jerusalem, although they also bought that land in the 1970s, the entire village is being demolished, and effluent from a nearby Palestinian town pours through their Area C land: environmental coercion is deliberately employed to displace them from the land they own.

Writing of the plight of the Bedouin, in a review of *High Hopes* in 2014, Noam Chomsky said: 'I visited the terrible Jahalin encampments near Ma'ale Adumim in 1996. The brutal uprooting of the Jahalin Bedouin in order to construct the illegal town of Ma'ale Adumim, virtually bisecting the West Bank, is one of the cruellest episodes of the unremitting Israeli violence perpetrated on their helpless Palestinian victims, while the world watches.' South African Nobel Prize winner, JM Coetzee, stated: 'I was all too familiar with the spectacle of so-called illegal settlements being bulldozed in South Africa of the apartheid years. Nevertheless, the relentless and ongoing destruction of Bedouin camps on the West Bank to make room for "legal" Israeli settlers tears at the heartstrings.'

The situation has only deteriorated since then.

Bedouin refugees in the West Bank claim their Right of Return to their lands inside Israel from which they were forcibly displaced in 1948 or the early 1950s. If they cannot return to Tel Arad in the Negev, they wish to remain where they are but would like to obtain planning permission there. Their minimal demand is for respect for their cultural needs and full consultation as to plans for their future: preferably by the Palestinian Authority (or by a future Palestinian state), not Israel's military. International humanitarian law demands that their full rights be respected, including those for FPIC – free, prior and informed consent before they are transferred from their lands.

In this battle for peace and normalcy for both Palestine and Israel, the rights of humanity, people's quality of life, and the added value of truth and justice are important to focus on, wherever that humanity is living. Or dying. As in Gaza. Deep breath. Keep calm, and carry on. A centred choice. Truth-seeking. Enlightenment. Consciousness raising. Compassion. A viable alternative to the militarism and neo-liberal capitalism that leaves so many behind. Each soul may find his or her own way towards that light, but one of many tests is always: 'Is this useful? Is this a place of growth? Does it go towards a greater love, a greater good? And does it spark inspiration, does it

High Hopes

benefit others?' Those questions are at the heart of Judaism, yet seem sadly absent in the political sphere, even of the religious right-wing.

I recall, thirty years ago, being stimulated to question and learn more when my teacher told me that my version of love was a very low-level affair and that a higher love exists. When I thought I was giving, was I actually needing to receive? Was I trying to enslave? Was my 'love' merely a form of possessiveness? Freedom implies letting go. A poem that I wrote in those days opened: 'The more you give, the more you get.'

These principles of freedom, of love and of 'turning the light' – of wilful hope, determined campaigning for peace and recognition that *life* is worth dying for, that freedom is one of the qualities of life without which life is not worth living, and that my quality of life cannot be whole or of consequence if it is at the expense of others' quality of life – these are some of the lessons learned during the ongoing period of apprenticeship. Even if one only occasionally registers the sacredness of life, its holistic nature and the incredibly magical gift of being – the privilege of inhabiting this miraculous planet – this awareness leaves an indelible mark that makes it impossible to walk away from the struggle for those values. Once you 'see' or 'get it' there is a responsibility implicit in that seeing. So, what are you going to *do* about it? And who in you needs or wants to? Where is the ego – what has to be let go, in order to receive?

It is all a never-ending battle, although the toolbox becomes more practised and mature. But the ego has its own ego-tricks, as all seekers or initiates know. Merely to overcome the zero-sum game of the Israeli government requires a strong spirit. In the psychological battle and militaristic game theory being waged by politicians and others in Israel-Palestine, we are being forced towards despair – as part of their strategy. We are encouraged to believe that there is no potential basis for peace and that we shall continue to dominate the Palestinians on the lands stretching from the Jordan River to the Mediterranean Sea.

But fighting back is also rooted in a deep concern with the future of Israel. Of the need for normal life for everyone between the River and the Sea. So, there is still no choice but to choose peace. The alternative is nihilistic, based on militarism and its bedfellows, fascism and chaos, which all too often create an escalating game that cannot achieve real security. For a country whose initial citizens were mainly refugees escaping from fascism, this is a tragic misdirection. We create what we fear, if we do not have sufficient awareness; abused families abuse, if not healed. Israel deserves a better fate than to be a modern Sparta.

Meeting these challenges is a spiritual necessity. We certainly don't have the luxury to walk away, once we have seen the other side. But while anger may be useful fuel for action, love seems to go deeper, with a greater ability to heal, to bring peace and to see inclusively with empathy and compassion – and perhaps less self-righteousness. This is how it is to walk 'in the other's shoes'.

Many seekers are drawn to desert, so much a focus of my own environmental activism: engendering a deep trust in the healing nature, simplicity, wonderful environment and special relationship of those desert dwellers to their ancient, pristine environment, coupled with an awareness even then, in the 1990s, of how fast the desert wilderness is being destroyed.

High Hopes

As the planet heats up, desert is fast advancing; but it is being transformed into real estate, not left virgin. Time may be running out. If we, nationals of the global village, cannot unite to protect and respect indigenous knowledge and wisdom, learned over thousands of years, especially as to how to live in extremes with grace, independence and love, how shall we cope with the overheating of the earth?

How shall we provide for the hopes and dreams that our children deserve, so that their lives be blessed, and fruitful, and 'normal'? Or will the children themselves be those who lead us out of the wilderness?

Note

1. A guidebook *Palestine & Palestinians* (Beit Sahour: Alternative Tourism Group) which I edited in 2002 allows people to explore through different means, as do my films: *Nowhere Left to Go, High Hopes* and *The Last Days of a School* (www.jahalin.org) which give voice to Bedouin facing displacement or those who have already been displaced.

Planting the Seeds of Home

Lubnah Shomali

I was born in Palestine, in 1972, in the small town of Beit Sahour in the West Bank after the Israeli occupation of the remainder of Mandatory Palestine in 1967. But even to describe the place I was born in is difficult. The importance of language cannot be understated – particularly in situations of conflict. The language or words used in the narrative describing a conflict – by the parties involved, by the international community and by the media – determines how the conflict is perceived. This, in turn, determines how the conflict will be addressed.

So when I say that I was born in Palestine – what does that mean? Am I indicating historic Palestine, the total of the land that was once under the British Mandate (1917–1948)? Or am I referencing the remainder of the land occupied by Israel in 1967? Or perhaps I am referring to only the West Bank, the area in which the Palestinian Authority has some measure of control?

The language used to describe the situation is of utmost importance. Firstly, it indicates which 'side' of the conflict you are on. But it is also elemental in developing and determining how you would solve the conflict. Even the term 'conflict' comes with its own baggage. When I hear the word 'conflict' it has a neutral connotation. It implies that the parties in conflict are on an equal footing and that the balance of power is distributed fairly between them. But this is not the case.

So my life can be plotted against language, which is contested. Just a few years before I came along was the 'Naksa', which means 'the smaller catastrophe'. It refers to the 1967 war in which Israel occupied the West Bank, the Gaza Strip and annexed East Jerusalem. We call this event smaller because less than twenty years before Palestinians experienced the 'Nakba', meaning 'the great catastrophe' of 1948. During the Nakba, at least seven hundred and fifty thousand Palestinians were forcibly displaced and dispossessed, the vast majority becoming refugees mainly in Jordan, Syria and Lebanon as well as in the remainder of Mandatory Palestine.[1] During the Naksa, approximately another five hundred thousand Palestinians experienced the same fate – some for a second time.

Most Israelis do not describe the past in this way. In fact it is even prohibited by Israeli law. For Israel, 1948 and 1967 are military and political victories, to be celebrated with parades, parties and fireworks. Accordingly, Israeli society applauds these military victories with little if any reference to the consequences on the Palestine people. The role played by Zionist militias (later absorbed into the Israeli military and government) and the Israeli government in dispersing and fragmenting the Palestinian people is minimised, if it is mentioned at all.

My father had studied in Egypt and received a degree in agricultural engineering. On returning to Palestine he became a teacher in three different schools in the Bethlehem area. He was a well-loved and respected teacher; I often encounter his former students who remember him fondly and speak well of him. He realised even then the limitations that would become the reality of our lives under Israeli oppression. My family chose not to remain in Palestine and we migrated to the United States in 1976.

Planting the Seeds of Home

Every parent strives to provide something better for their children. By leaving Palestine for the USA my father chose the best option to provide a better life for us: a better house, education, health care and family life. We lived in a Palestinian community. Our life in the States wasn't bad; initially we struggled financially but eventually our economic situation improved. I should highlight here that my family went to the United States as immigrants – not refugees. In other words, we went by choice not by force. This is very important as the legal status and what is provided by the host state varies between refugee and immigrant. But even though we were immigrants and not refugees there was always something missing, or off, about our period in the States. The dispossessed are often haunted with the past; what they left behind, their memories, their loved ones, their lands, their lives. They live in limbo going through the routines and rituals of the present while longing for a return home. There is a constant homesickness, a feeling of being incomplete – especially for those who were forced out and denied return. And our family was no exception. In 1949, then Prime Minister of Israel, David Ben-Gurion said, 'We must do everything to ensure they [the Palestinians] never do return … The old will die and the young will forget.'[2] However, this was not the case – not for the Palestinian refugees, and not for us. My father was particularly adamant about remembering, visiting and returning to Palestine.

Fortunately, for us, it was possible to return (another stark difference between an immigrant and refugee) and we did quite often for summer visits. These visits were happy times, filled with family occasions and events when we saw the best Palestine had to offer and the changes wrought by Israel. It's interesting to visit a place multiple times over a period of three decades: changes are much more easily observed. The encroachment of the Israeli 'settlements' onto Palestinian land, the restrictions, the suppression and dehumanisation of the people, the tensions and the uncertainty increased with each visit. These visits were also essential in shaping our relationship with Palestine, both the land and the people. Our identities were developed and solidified through the intensive exposure into Palestinian life, culture and traditions. This was the main driver behind my father's insistence for the visits: to plant the seeds of home in our hearts and minds.

It might seem that we are a very political family, but we are not. However, our daily life is the 'settlements', the checkpoints and the legal system which controls our every move – so we observe, comment on and live in the conflict. My husband, at one point in his life, was active in the resistance, before and during the first intifada (also known as the Stone Throwers' Uprising). He was detained by the Israeli military many times – overall he spent around three years in Israeli prisons – a fate the vast majority of Palestinian men (and ever increasingly women) share. As a teenager, when my husband was not quite seventeen, before the first intifada, the local district commander from the Israeli army was making his rounds. While riding his bicycle, my husband decided he would throw stones at him. The commander gave chase and caught him. They arrested him and beat him so badly that he was hospitalised. Then they decided to evict the whole family from their home.

In international law – particularly the Fourth Geneva Convention – it is illegal to forcibly transfer someone from

Planting the Seeds of Home

one part of an occupied territory to another. Also it is illegal to impose collective punishment on people for what they did not do. But despite these two very clear legal standards the goal was to maximise control of the area with the minimum number of Palestinians living in it – suppression of resistance against this goal was the means to this end. The military trucks came and the family was forced to load everything onto the trucks and they and their belongings were dumped in Jericho, out in the heart, and the heat, of the desert.

Although they were left in the desert Palestinians there offered them a home. Many people knew my late father-in-law because he was a civil society leader. He would often write articles for newspapers and give speeches at demonstrations. But he refused this hospitality knowing that if he 'settled' in a home in Jericho the possibility to return to Beit Sahour would diminish significantly. Instead, he invited the media to come and see what the army had done to them and he campaigned in this way to bring about their return home. Fortunately, it worked, the media coverage, both local and international, pressured Israel to allow their return.

This was the life that created my husband's decision to become active in the Palestinian resistance. It is not we who are political but our circumstances condemn us to politics. Even simple things – like which words we choose to describe our life – carry political connotations. Each word has so many facets, so many dimensions: the legal, political, and national connotations. Let's take 'settlements' for example. Creating 'settlements' in occupied territory or in strict legal jargon, the implantation of the civilian population of the occupier in the occupied territory, is against international law.³ This crime should activate the obligations of third parties to act to rectify the situation.

But the use of the word 'settlement' contributes to the international negligence in this regard. The term 'settlement' is legally neutral; in other words it does not bear any negative legal connotation or positive legal obligation (even if the act itself is prohibited). It is also literally positive: it implies returning to a place of rest or planting roots. The use of this term by the world invokes the positive connotations and re-enforces a narrative frame which says that Israelis are 'returning to their land'. Yet international law also provides an alternative language which frames the implantation of Israeli civilians on Palestinian land in terms of oppression and justice: colonialism.

But use of the word 'colonialism' comes at a great cost to the world. This is why there is hesitancy, or even outright refusal, to use this term. Such an acknowledgement bears significant legal consequences for the international community: third parties to the conflict would be obligated to intervene to rectify such a scenario and there would be significant penalties imposed on the perpetrator. The legal downplay, or misrepresentation, of the reality in Palestine, creates a justification for the prohibited actions carried out by Israel but also provides impunity for these actions.

'Settlements' are a very clear example of this. The world acknowledges that 'settlements' are illegal. Political leaders often describe them as one of the 'main obstacles to peace'; yet, little is done to slow or halt their expansion. The international political will to act against 'settlements' does not exist and so they proliferate unabashed. The question to ask then is how can

Planting the Seeds of Home

we change the political will? Continuing to use the same bland and inconsequential terminology to describe Israel's actions and the reality on the ground only exacerbates the situation by providing a veil of false approval and acquiescence. Without a valid diagnosis, we cannot begin to administer the correct medicine. Only when the reality of the situation in Palestine is narrated utilising the applicable terminology can we begin to address and rectify the situation successfully.

This is why I prefer to use the word 'colony' to describe the Israeli project of uprooting Palestinians from their land and building towns full of people where once there were farms or villages. Colony, or the act of creating and supporting colonies (aka colonialism or colonisation), has definitive legal consequences and it accurately describes the moral and political framework of our lives.

On the ground the ever-expanding Israeli colonial enterprise translates into a deplorable situation for the remaining Palestinian population. The fragmentation and dispersion of the Palestinian people also increases. Families and communities have and continue to be fragmented; torn apart by not only the Nakba and the Naksa, but the ongoing displacement and dispossession that is still occurring today. This is coupled with the ongoing denial of the right of refugees to return. There isn't a single Palestinian family that has been left whole or untouched by this fragmentation.

My own family has relatives all over the world; Europe, the United States, Jordan, Lebanon and Syria, some who left like us as immigrants, some who were forced to flee, and some who attempted to return and were not allowed. My husband has seven siblings; throughout the years when they have wanted to see each other they must do it in Jordan. When my father and mother-in-law passed away (each separately) not all their children could attend the funeral. When my husband's twenty-year-old nephew died in a bus accident in Syria (he was studying there in 2003) some members of the family were also prevented from attending the funeral in Palestine. These are just but some examples of how families are kept from grieving together.

We are also prevented from celebrating together on such important occasions as graduations, weddings, and the birth of new family members. The whole construct of family and social life is disrupted. Rather than lessening or reducing family bonds and relations, however, we are more determined to make sure family and social life are prioritised. We make special and consistent efforts to be a part of both celebrations and sad occasions – and part of just everyday life.

People believed that the Oslo Accords (1993 and 1995) represented a path to peace, stability and justice. But none of those words can be used in the same sentence as Oslo – at least not in their proper and true meaning. The stability that was established was the entrenchment of the occupation and continuing land grab. The peace was polluted by increased Israeli state-sponsored violence, security coordination with the Palestinian Authority and intensification of the suppression of the people. And justice? That word is foreign to the Oslo Accords. As the time passed after Oslo and the reality set in, the hope dissipated and was replaced with frustration, resentment and fear; so, many withdrew from political life, at least from the historic Palestinian parties. And yes, there existed many more

Planting the Seeds of Home

political parties than just Fatah and Hamas; but all of them lost their influence and legitimacy. Palestinians are still identified by which party they affiliated with historically but to claim that any political party has the support of the masses is erroneous.

Both the Oslo Accords (1993 and 1995) provided administrative measures to manage rather than resolve the conflict by addressing the root causes and were based on the significant imbalance of power between the Palestinians and Israel. My husband (and many others) rejected the Oslo Accords from the beginning; so much so that he preferred to leave Palestine than to stay when in 1995 Yasser Arafat and the PLO 'returned' triumphantly to still occupied Palestine. He definitely did not consider Oslo to be a viable solution or a pathway to peace. He felt it constituted a compromise of the inalienable rights of the Palestinian people, a sell out by the Palestinian leadership.

Today my husband has taken a decision to withdraw from politics and from activism. Yet despite this, sharing my father's outlook, we, my husband, my three children and I embarked on a more permanent return to our little hometown of Beit Sahour in 2008.

The common reaction to this decision was priceless: the extremely perplexed look and responses ranged from the fairly mild inquiry of 'why?' to the brutal 'are you crazy?' Interestingly enough this was the response from our Palestinian friends and relatives as well as American and European friends. Of course there was the timing: our move came after what has now been dubbed the second intifada from 2000 to 2005; the sound defeat of Israel by Hezbollah in the 2006 Lebanon War; and the split in the Palestinian Authority between Fatah and Hamas in 2007.

We understood why people would be concerned for our safety. But, for us, we were racing against time. Soon our children would be far too settled into their lives in the US and too old to adapt to a different language, culture and life. More importantly, we wanted to plant the seeds of home, their real home in Palestine.

I wish I could say it was easy; I wish I could say that I have no doubts that we did the right thing; I wish I could say I have no regrets. But I can't say any of those things. Our first Christmas in Palestine we spent glued to the television watching the Israeli war on Gaza (2008–2009). My children were young and scared; they would ask 'are we safe?' and I would lie and say 'yes'. And they would ask 'how do you know?' and 'are you sure?' I don't remember exactly what I said but somehow I reassured them with what I am sure were half-truths. Amazingly, we witnessed all three wars against our people in Gaza; frustrated, weeping and astounded that something so inhumane could occur not once, not twice, but, three times. With each war international solidarity with the Palestinian people would surge and so would hope: demonstrations in the capitals of many countries, petitions, calls for justice. And then, the failure of the international community to address the deplorable situation in Gaza and the rest of Palestine resulted in even more disappointment. Today we live with the idea that war on Gaza could happen anytime; it's a permanent possibility hovering in the back of our minds.

It may seem that all these things are separate and disconnected. But look beyond the surface and the words: the dispossession, the suppression, the wars, the colonies, the land grab, the imprisonment, the denial of return, all of them buttress a greater

Planting the Seeds of Home

purpose. All these actions and many, many more translate into the denial of life, liberties and fundamental rights of the Palestinian people. In many cases, these acts are considered war crimes or crimes against humanity under international law.[4] Accordingly, when these types of acts are committed the international community is obligated to respond in ways that would halt and prevent them from happening. Unfortunately, aside from minimal condemnation of these acts, very little has been done to thwart the continued human rights violations and crimes perpetrated against the Palestinian people. Choosing not to respond or to respond with inappropriate measures, like enhancing relations with Israel, has served to bolster Israeli confidence. Israel is led to believe that any act of aggression, and the continued displacement and dispossession are permissible. While the international community is quick to respond to other states' aggressions and violations, they tread on eggshells around Israel; barely fulfilling their minimum obligations towards the Palestinian people to ensure that they can live in peace and security.

When can true and lasting peace be achieved? In my opinion, it is when we apply international law even-handedly and ensure the rights of all peoples. This requires that we examine conflicts in an unbiased way, through a rights-based approach that takes into consideration the lives of the people most affected and not the political and economic interest of states. This means that we must be prepared and willing to hold states that violate the law accountable. There is something to be gained from continued upheaval and conflict in the Middle East for states; the continued power imbalance and domination of the region by foreign powers. So naturally states would be unwilling to relinquish the benefits that they gain from controlling a region or a people. But there is so much more to be gained through peace with justice. Not the sugar-coated false justice that we have experienced with Oslo and the 'peace process'. But true peace, the kind that sets the foundations for reconciliation, development, equality and the ever-elusive pursuit of happiness can only be achieved when it is coupled with justice.

In June of 2018 we complete nine consecutive years living in Palestine. My children are much older now, on the verge of young adulthood. During this time I have tried to educate them both academically and in other ways. Palestinian culture places significant importance on academic education. Education was, and continues to be, perceived by Palestinians as a necessity for achieving a good quality of life but also as a mechanism of liberation. In other words, only an educated, informed and active civil society could successfully liberate Palestine from foreign domination and oppression. This belief was instilled in me by my father. He had studied in Egypt and received a degree in agricultural engineering. During that time, the 1950s and 1960s, Palestinians usually pursued their higher education abroad as there weren't many universities in Palestine. He made sure that I received a BA and MBA in the US. My children are being educated in Palestine. My oldest daughter is studying marketing at Birzeit University, close to Ramallah.

In addition to their traditional education, I hope that they have been educated in other ways. They have developed relationships with other Palestinians and the many people from around the world who work in Palestine. They have become aware of the cultural and traditional norms of our people. They have selectively enjoyed, embraced, frowned upon and rejected different experiences. They have seen up close and personal what it means to be dominated by a foreign power. They have experienced love, joy, pain, sadness, loss, friendship, and family in the unique way that only Palestine can provide. It is my hope that they have taken from these experiences what they need to develop their characters and principles on solid first-hand knowledge that will shape their identity and consciousness. This is my hope for them.

Sometimes I am overwhelmed. Sometimes the sense of loss is so great that I fall into despair and hopelessness. How is it that we can continue under these circumstances? How can we move forward? Well, at this stage that's not what's required. For now it's not about moving forward, for the deck is stacked – and it's in Israel's favour. The strategy for now is to hold; to stay the course. This situation, resulting in the suffocation of life, land and fundamental freedoms could potentially break the people. But it hasn't. Perhaps on the surface it looks like determination, has turned to surrender; apathy replaced passion; fragmentation replaced unity; despair replaced hope. But as always we need to look beyond the surface, look deeper. Look past the rift between Fatah and Hamas, look past the defunct Palestinian Liberation Organisation, look past Israel's hasbara and Trump's blustering, look past the pathetic luke-warm response of the international community; the Palestinian people are still here. Against all these obstacles, amidst all the chaos, and the contextual noise, the Palestinian people remain steadfast and their voice is loud and clear. We are here and we will remain and we will return.

DEFENDING HOPE

Notes

1. Palestine was a Class A mandate under the British from 1917–1948.
2. Karma Nabulsi, 'The Great Catastrophe', *The Guardian*, 12 May 2006. www.theguardian.com/world/2006/may/12/israel1/.
3. The Declaration on the Granting of Independence to Colonial Countries and Peoples, adopted by General Assembly resolution 1514 (XV) of 14 December 1960, defines and prohibits colonialism and colonization. While only a UN resolution, the Declaration has gained the status of customary international law, meaning it is obligatory on all States. Or in other words, the prohibition of colonialism is a peremptory norm of international law.
4. According to The Hague Regulations of 1907, the Geneva Conventions (especially the Fourth Geneva Convention), the Universal Declaration of Human Rights and many more international treaties and resolutions.

The Long-Distance Run to Freedom

Sari Bashi

Pursuing the two passions of my life – human rights and long-distance running – has taught me to appreciate the beauty of human beings and human struggles.

For the past decade, my commitment to defending the right to freedom of movement for Palestinian residents of Gaza has blossomed with my passion for running very long distances, up to and including a two hundred and sixteen kilometre trail race. In my professional life, I try to free those who are trapped, and in my personal life, I celebrate the liberty of moving my body through space.

I started running long distances in 2005, the year I turned thirty, the year my co-founder, Kenneth Mann, and I established Gisha, and the year the Israeli government withdrew its permanent military ground presence in the Gaza Strip, removed Jewish settlements and closed Gaza's crossings.

I moved to Tel Aviv to work with Kenneth on a project aimed at protecting the freedom of movement of Gaza residents. I sat in Kenneth's law office, and with his help, began writing letters to the Israeli military, court petitions, grant applications and news releases. We focused on freedom of movement because, in our view, access restrictions had become the dominant means of oppression employed by the Israeli occupation. Every day, restrictions on travel and transfer of goods limit the horizons of hundreds of thousands of Palestinians, mostly those against whom even the Israeli authorities make no security allegations.

The problem is urgent, and the solution is mutually beneficial, because Israeli society gains nothing from blocking its neighbours from pursuing their dreams.

We focused on Gaza, because the Israeli 'disengagement', as it was called, created a new set of access restrictions. Israeli soldiers were no longer restricting movement inside Gaza, but they were patrolling the perimeter, preventing people from travelling between Gaza, Israel and the West Bank and blocking goods from entering and leaving. Unemployment rose, as farmers and manufacturers were prevented from transferring goods to external markets. Shortages developed, as the Israeli defence ministry used mathematical formulae to limit the kinds and quantities of supplies to the minimum needed for Gaza's basic humanitarian needs. New procedures prevented family reunification between Gaza and the West Bank.

The logic of the disengagement, for the Israeli government, was to disengage from responsibility for life inside Gaza – while continuing to control movement. Years of restrictions meant that most Israelis no longer knew Palestinians from Gaza, and most young people in Gaza had never left the Strip. Demonisation of the Other ran high on both sides, and the government successfully promoted a narrative, flawed factually but captivating for the public, that 'we left Gaza, and they fired rockets at us'.

We needed to present a counter-narrative, one that promoted accountability for continued Israeli control of movement into and out of Gaza. We needed to expose violations of human rights that destroyed families and choked normal life. We did not want to reinforce images of Palestinians in the Israeli and

The Long-Distance Run to Freedom

Western media as either perpetrators of violence or victims of oppression, images that alienate rather than foster empathy. We wanted to focus on the beautiful human potential that would be released if students were allowed to reach their studies, workers to get to their jobs, and families to build lives together.

I had Kenneth's encouragement, advice, and office space. I had a fellowship from Yale Law School that allowed me to devote my time to this new project that we called 'Gisha', the Hebrew word for access. Clients from Gaza began to call, hearing through word of mouth that a new organisation was willing to help. But I wasn't sure how to make my vision a reality.

And then one day, I saw a programme on the internet, an Excel table for marathon training: run such-and-such number of kilometres each day, and within four months you'll reach a marathon. Compared to trying to remove obstacles to people travelling into and out of Gaza, when it came to running, the goal and path seemed simple. I started representing Palestinian residents of Gaza in Israeli courts, and I started running distances that became increasingly longer.

Ever since then, running has been an integral part of my work and my commitment to freedom of movement. Through long-distance running, I discovered the calm that comes with effort. The sensation of my feet touching the ground, one after the other, was a repetitive action that put me in a meditative state. Sometimes I ran to release frustration – struggles against the army, courtroom losses, clients we couldn't help. Sometimes I ran to work out some legal manoeuvre in my head. Sometimes I ran just to celebrate movement through space – crossing city limits, passing through parks, forests and orchards. After running dozens of kilometres, after you get past the heaviness and fatigue of the beginning, the body and soul enter a state of lightness. The only limitation was the strength in my legs and the amount of food and water I carried. As the distances got longer, I discovered something amazing – we human beings are capable of much more than we think. And much more than others think of us.

When running races of one hundred, one hundred and sixty or two hundred and sixteen kilometres, you don't look good. You don't feel strong. You become intimately aware of how weak your muscles are as they struggle to pump you up a hill, how fragile your digestive system is, as it tries to process the energy to continue, and how duplicitous your mind is, as it floods you with self-doubt. Your skin is coated with dirt and sweat, your eyes are red from lack of sleep, and your gait is awkward and halting. And yet the perseverance to continue to the finish line contains more beauty than a supermodel posing on a white-sand beach. The humble act of human striving is simply, blindingly beautiful.

I won races by embracing the struggle to continue forward. And in my work, I removed crippling restrictions on movement by persevering and calling attention to the beauty of human achievement.

The dichotomy between difficulty and transcendence has been a central tension in my life as both a runner and a lawyer. Navigating this tension is the point where hope, progress and success have flourished. Most days, human rights work doesn't feel good. It's hard. We take on systems of oppression and injustice daily, and we do so from a position of weakness, advocating for unpopular causes and the dignity of those seen as the enemy. We lose more often than we win. We are seen as enemies, foreigners in our own societies, naïve, disconnected and dangerous. Yet the beauty of our struggle is pure and real because it is so deeply human. The halting progress we make is like a diamond shimmering within the dark cave of human frailty.

I recall one case in particular where I experienced the power of hope, even as human rights were being trampled upon. In 2008, the Gaza Strip was sealed almost hermetically. For a brief period, Israel ran shuttle buses to allow at least some students, enrolled in foreign universities, to leave Gaza by transiting through Israel and the West Bank, to the airport in Jordan. But then that stopped, too. I called a reporter trying to draw media attention to the fact that students were trapped in Gaza.

'Everyone is trapped in Gaza,' he said. 'That's not news.'

We kept trying. We filed court petitions on behalf of individual students, published a report and initiated a hearing in the Knesset, the Israeli parliament, chaired by a rabbi who invoked the Jewish people's reputation as 'the people of the book' to enjoin the defence minister to let the students travel.

Then we became aware that the American government was cancelling scholarships awarded to Palestinian students in Gaza as part of its prestigious Fulbright study-abroad programme, because Israel refused to allow them to leave the Strip. What could be more admirable than gifted young people invited to attend universities with tuition paid by American taxpayers? What could be more different from the image of Gaza residents that so many in Israel and the West have – of faceless people who are either dangerous or wretched?

DEFENDING HOPE

I convinced that same reporter to write a story, which made it to the front page of *The New York Times*, about how the United States of America was rescinding scholarships awarded under its flagship international exchange programme because it could not persuade its closest ally in the Middle East to allow seven of Gaza's brightest young people to reach their universities in the United States. Within hours, the news reached then-secretary of state Condoleezza Rice, who was asked why Fulbright scholarships were being cancelled for Palestinian students. She answered that, in her opinion, that was a bad idea. And it was.

Within forty-eight hours, the government of Israel agreed to allow not just the Fulbright scholars to leave Gaza, but hundreds more students who needed to get to universities abroad. More important than the localised victory was the paradigm shift – in Jerusalem and in Washington, decision-makers and standard-bearers began to see the potential that was being suppressed by the sweeping travel restrictions.

Human rights activists inside Israel face many dilemmas. Our community wants to expose the ugliness of the occupation and to demand accountability. But we must do this while also reminding the Israeli public of the stunning beauty of upholding human rights and freedom. It is this beauty for which we all strive, and it is a tool for motivating, rallying and ultimately pointing the way forward. If we want to motivate people to action, we must expose the ugliness of military occupation in a way that leaves space for hope. And we must do so in recognition that our race is a long-distance one.

This is what has dictated my choices about strategy and pace. To finish a two hundred and sixteen kilometre run, you have to be aware of where you are. The twentieth kilometre isn't the right place to try a short sprint that will give you a few minutes' edge on your finishing time. You'll pay the price for it later. And dearly.

My very first clients were a group of ten students from Gaza who had been studying occupational therapy by remote control – video conferencing, email and the occasional visit from a foreign lecturer – because Israel refused to allow them to reach the only Palestinian occupational therapy degree programme, at Bethlehem University in the West Bank. It was September 2005. I submitted court petitions on behalf of each student, hoping that they would be allowed to reach their studies by the start of the winter semester. The proceedings dragged on for two years and ended in the petition being rejected. After Gisha launched two more legal and public campaigns to end the ban on students from Gaza studying in the West Bank. At times we seemed very close to succeeding, garnering support from influential Israeli academics and public figures, getting supreme court judges to pressure the state, obtaining widespread and favourable media coverage inside and outside Israel. Each time, we ultimately failed to overturn the ban. And each time, we learned something more about the nature of the obstacle – about the changes we needed to create, within the Israeli defence ministry and the international and local community exerting pressure on it – in order to allow Palestinian students from Gaza to access Palestinian universities in the West Bank. Toward the end of each court case, we sprinted forward, only to learn that the finish line was further away than we thought.

In the fight to protect Gaza residents, we have to remember where we are – with respect to the Israeli public, the Israeli justice system and the geopolitical context. Today, we are fighting for basic norms of humanity. Before we can succeed in making human rights a reality for Gaza residents, we first have to remind the Israeli public that Gaza residents are human beings. Unfortunately, this isn't self-evident. If we are going to move forward, we need to start from the place we are now, even if it's not where we would like to be.

I recall a coaching session in which Gisha's spokesperson helped me prepare for a radio interview about Palestinians from Gaza being arrested and forcibly removed from the West Bank, as part of Israel's policy to restrict travel between the two parts of the Palestinian territory.

'Soldiers are arresting students, workers, husbands and wives and tearing them away from their homes,' I said in the practice session. She frowned.

'Don't say that soldiers are doing the arresting,' she said.

'Why not?' I asked.

'Because it's too hard for people to hear. Soldiers are viewed positively, and if you open by asking people to believe that soldiers are doing something bad, they will respond by tuning you out as a radical. Start with the people being affected – families separated – explain what is happening to them, and let listeners feel empathy for them. After listeners are drawn in, they will understand that it is the soldiers who are doing the arresting.'

She reminded me to start from where we human rights activists stand in relation to the society whose behaviour we are trying to change – not where we wish we stood.

That sober, honest recognition of our relative weakness has been a tremendous source of strength for me. I remember how

The Long-Distance Run to Freedom

scared I was when I got the state's response to my first series of court petitions, on behalf of those ambitious young people from Gaza trying to further their occupational therapy studies. The fax machine spat out twenty-seven pages of military orders, court precedent and political decisions that obliterated any semblance of individuality or justice. I was up against the Israeli Shin Bet, the government of Israel, and the Israeli military commander in charge of the West Bank, and I was fighting them in an Israeli court. I felt intimidated, powerless, and weak. That was the time when I started running marathons. That was the time when I began to collect, in my muscle memory, the experience of overcoming my own physical weakness, in order to reach the finish line. That was the time when I began to define strength as feeling my weakest – and pushing forward anyway.

I still get scared sometimes, when facing the seemingly absolute power of a military occupation. I still feel anxious when I see how far away our goals are, of a world in which human rights are respected. But in facing setbacks, I take a deep breath, smile, and remember that this is only the beginning of a very long struggle. I try to be gentle with myself and my colleagues and partners. I remind them that we need to preserve our strength. This is not a sprint.

To See the Sun Rise Again

Raji Sourani

My dearest Basal,

To be a human rights defender you must be a kind of romantic revolutionary. You have to believe in the justness of your cause when all the circumstances tell you to abandon it. You have to believe with resolve that justice will triumph even when the world around you is bleak. The world your Mum and I have brought you into is indeed bleak. As you have grown from baby, to boy, to man – it has become nothing but bleaker. For me this reflects a kind of unfulfilled aspect of my life: everything I did was insufficient to overcome what was thrown at me, at us – as Palestinians. I wanted you to grow up proud as a free Palestinian. But I have not been able to give you this. I wanted you to have the chemistry of visiting your cousins in the West Bank, of touching the history of Jerusalem and swimming in the sea in Haifa. But that life was never available for you. Instead, I can only offer you the hope that as you enter your adult life, as a lawyer, your desire for justice will burn as brightly as my own. Perhaps your children will enjoy the freedom you never had.

The bleakness of the world never nullified my desire for justice. As the bleakness grows, in fact, I have set store in the things which pain has taught as well as those things which joy has offered me. Khalil Gibran, the great Lebanese poet, reminds us that no matter what problems come you should face the future with the same unwavering commitment: with beauty in your heart and with belief in what is true.

DEFENDING **HOPE**

Throughout my life I have been able to keep these views despite the tests that I faced. I am a very reconciled person; by reconciled I mean that I am complete in my views and follow through on what I know is true, irrespective of the cost. But the cost was sometimes very, very heavy and my inner resolve was so often tested. It seems like the life given to us Palestinians is that of a prison complex and we must unlock many doors before we can leave.

The first time I was tortured was a shock. I had been a lawyer for many years. I would visit clients in prison and they would tell me they were victims of torture. I would inspect them for marks, scars and any physical signs of torture. If I did not see any marks I would discount what they said. For many years I continued this practice. One day I was in Gaza's central military prison visiting some clients. As I came to the last visit I was approached by one of the guards who said that the visitation time was over.

'We have an emergency situation. You have to leave the prison,' he said.

I left through a side door but as I did two members of the secret service (Shabak) and two prison guards appeared behind me. I continued walking towards the exit when one of them called to me.

Despite my protestations that I was a lawyer visiting clients they didn't allow me to leave. Instead they took me with my suit, with my tie, with my bag. They took me directly from there to the interrogation department. They insisted on hooding me but I refused. I tried to argue, demanding to know if I had been arrested or not.

But they would not say. I continued to resist and to insist on calling my wife. But in the end they put the hood on me and put me briefly inside one of the rooms. Waiting for me were six or seven other secret service people. They began to shout as if they had caught the big head of an organisation – and this was in a time when I went almost daily to the prison, my whereabouts were not unknown to them.

They began to taunt me with the prospect of a lifetime in prison, and they began to enjoy themselves, creating a celebratory atmosphere. After half an hour, I asked them for a moment to speak. I reiterated my demand to know what my legal status was at that moment.

The answer was simple: my fate was in my hands. If I agree to become a collaborator then I would be free to walk away in a few minutes. If I refused then I would be imprisoned.

I knew that collaboration was not a life of freedom. And I trusted my ability to withstand their torture because of my unwavering faith in the justness of our cause. I also knew that they had no legal grounds to detain me for any length but that many before me had been convicted on less evidence.

After speaking, they were mad at me. Two minutes later, the boss, the head of the secret service in Gaza, came in. His name was Abu Ammar. He spoke to the other guards as if he had been watching proceedings, probably from behind a two-way mirror.

He threatened me more until eventually he warned me: 'Raji, we will crush your skull.' He ordered his men to take me elsewhere and to force me to confess.

This was when the real interrogation began. The torture was both physical and psychological. To start with they hooded and handcuffed me for twenty-four hours. During this time I was not allowed to sleep, or to sit, or to even lean against the wall. As the night turned I began to collapse and to have a very severe headache. This was the first time I decided to sit, thinking that I have nothing to lose. I could not tolerate my headache anymore and my body could not tolerate standing up. So I decided to sit. They came in and began to beat me while sitting down. Then they forced me to stand up, so I stood up. After half an hour, the same thing happened. I could not stand up so I sat again and they began beating me. Eventually, I stood up. Then I began to shout at them, cursing them. Then the officer came in and asked them to bring me to his office.

So I went, though I was just about able to stand – of course handcuffed and torn. They took the hood from my head. My eyes took some time to readjust and function properly but I could see him sitting behind his desk. He leaned back in his chair and placed his feet on the table. He took a relaxed and friendly tone which was designed to disconcert me further.

I told him that I could not stand. My head was pounding and that I needed rest. He took this opportunity to ask me to confess. He even offered to remove my handcuffs so I could write a confession. I had not been charged with any crime so I could not confess to any crime.

At this point I was unbalanced, nothing seemed clear. I could not think straight but I did not want to give this man the satisfaction of breaking me. I composed myself as best I could though my head was still throbbing. I tried to relax in the chair even though I could feel my body just wanted to collapse. I spoke to him in the firmest, loudest voice I could find in my broken body and I shouted abuse at him. I called him names and insulted his family, really whatever I could think of.

Anyone who ever spent time in prison knows that the worst possible thing to do is to shout obscene curses at an officer. But to curse at an officer of the Shabak, in the middle of the interrogation department in their Gaza headquarters, is like signing your own death warrant. To this day I still think it was one of the craziest things I ever did. I remember so clearly the look in his eyes, wide with disbelief. For a long time he just stared at me. He was absolutely stunned. I knew that inside he was in rage and turmoil. Interrogation is a power game and the last resort of the powerless is to seek some sort of power over the interrogator. This is why I cursed him. But of course the power always lies with him, who has an army at his disposal, who can beat me and keep me in prison without anyone ever knowing, who can go and threaten and injure my family. He took off one of his shoes and he moved fast along the table and he came for me. He spat in my face. Then he began to hit me with his shoe. He began shouting and screaming at me while swinging wildly with his shoe on my face and my body. A number of guards came in because of the commotion.

He spoke two words that sealed my fate: 'crucify him'.

I didn't know what this meant and I hardly had the presence of mind to think about it before a number of guards picked me up. They took me to a doorway. They had some sort of contraption with an iron bar in it going through either side of the doorway and they lifted me up and tied me to the iron bar. I recall that I began to shout, to curse, to kick the door, but after that, I lost consciousness. The next morning I remember somebody kicking me slightly with his foot while softly calling my name. He asked if I needed food. I didn't. He asked if I needed water. I didn't. He asked if I needed the toilet. I did. So he took me. I was in the bathroom for five minutes when someone came in and asked if I would eat something.

So, I ate a little. Then they resumed the interrogation and this went on, and on, for fifty-eight days. Every day I wished to die, every day, more than twenty times. Every day I was interrogated three or four times. I was both mentally and physically exhausted. They kept insisting that I confess. I asked them what I should confess to and they told me to make something up.

Eventually, they brought charges to me that would have resulted in me spending twenty years in prison. The American Bar Association and Amnesty International took up my case, campaigning for me as a prisoner of conscience. Then the Shabak decided to send me to administrative detention. Under the administrative detention system all the information is secret and the only ones who know the charges are the prosecuting lawyer, the representative of the Judge Advocate General (JAG) and the judge. You can't defend yourself against the evidence or the charges. It is like confronting a ghost. Despite this, I was sentenced to three years for doing nothing. Yet I felt like one of the really lucky ones. For all the hell I went through psychologically and physically prison became a time of transformation for me.

I had already discovered a lot professionally as to how the system works: the intricate relationships between the secret services, the police, the JAG and the court, from the inside. That enriched my perspective as a lawyer quite a lot. (Of course I'm not suggesting that every lawyer should go to the prison for their training, although there are some who would appreciate that!) Instead, I understood how the law could be used as a tool of oppression. After all it was the Landau Commission that turned Israel into the first country in the world to de facto legalise torture by allowing 'moderate physical pressure'. In other words, instead of burning us at the stake they burnt us with the bureaucracy. And so I understood that the law – for which I have full respect – is not a sacred object but is subject to human manipulation.

But can you imagine that in these moments of torture and extreme physical discomfort somewhere in my mind lurked the idea that human rights law could restore my dignity. It may seem hard to imagine that an abstract idea has this power but in such desperate times the desperate will rely on anything to give them hope. Throughout the times they tortured me I believed I had the moral superiority and everything they did to me reassured me of that. Hard times push you to give up or to stand up for each other. You have no right to give up.

I decided to use every second of my imprisonment in a positive way. When I was outside prison I didn't sleep: there was always politics, work, something to do. But in prison I began to sleep in the best way ever in my life, like a baby. And I ate: usually I didn't take the time to eat properly, instead grabbing some food while on the run from one place to another (even with your grandmother's famous *bamia*!). But in prison I ate three meals a day. I took the time to enjoy the company, sharing food with my cellmates. I was happy to talk, to learn, to look into people's faces – to really search their eyes. I loved to listen to people's stories and see how they walked. I became an observer of people, taking the time to watch them and study them. I saw the very cool ones, the ones with many problems in their lives outside and the different ways they would react. I understood from my observations that human beings are not uniform in their perspectives towards life.

I was lucky: although I worried about my family and how they were living I also took the approach that I could do nothing about it.

'I am in here. They are out there.'

Accepting this allowed me the space to make some major decisions. The most important of those was to learn Hebrew. I decided that I could not work in politics or the law without a powerful command of Hebrew. So I began to read everything I could find in Hebrew. I learned the Hebrew dialect of my prison guards. Then I studied the regulations of the occupation, of the Egyptians and Jordanians until 1967, the regulations of the British until 1948 and of the Ottoman Empire before them. Everything I learned in Hebrew. I would spend time with the Geneva Conventions writing out each article and the Commentaries: all in Hebrew. We could access all these books in the library or else we could pay the guards to let people smuggle them into us. I also began to read extensively in English – reading the classics, reading Russian literature, much of it smuggled from the outside. It was a real landmark point in my life: devouring food, knowledge, sleep and the company of good friends. From day one I was preparing myself mentally and physically for going back out into the world. It was not an easy battle but I was sitting at my meals beside people who had ten life sentences imposed on them. They would say to me:

'Raji, what is it, three years? It is nothing. It is tomorrow.'

Their views were a gift to me. They gave me the perspective of time, thus understanding how to think long-term and strategically. I asked myself: 'What preparations do I need to make in here for unforeseen events in the years to come?' The alternative was to be sad, to be angry and to feel rough in your heart and your body. In some ways that was the easy choice but it was also the ugly choice.

I learned also that the nature of people is not fixed or pre-determined. Our enemy is not another people but it is an ideology: Zionism. Even those people who embrace this ideology have the capacity to change. Zionism has conquered the fearful hearts of many Israelis. But there are also many who are not controlled by this ideology who can see the humanity in others.

While I was in solitary confinement there was an Israeli prison guard who would smuggle me cigarettes. At first I rejected them and threw them back at him so that I could not be manipulated for information. But then one night he slipped a copy of the *National Geographic* under my door. In it was a photo-spread about the Swiss Alps. For a prisoner with no place to go, to see photographs of the spaciousness of the mountains was transformative. I could dream of other places and imagine that I was a bird soaring through the air in freedom. From that day on I realised that his advances were good natured and I allowed him to help me through dark days. Although he was a prison guard and although he was an Israeli, he was simply another human trying to find his way in this world.

It was people like him who reaffirmed the correctness of our path to me. This man was a human being trapped by an ideology that had dehumanised us as Palestinians but he had travelled beyond it. We could see beyond the cells to the humanity of the Other. As the poet Samih al Qasim writes:

> From the narrow window of my small cell,
> I see trees that are smiling at me
> and rooftops crowded with my family.
> And windows weeping and praying for me.
> From the narrow window of my small cell –
> I can see your big cell!
>
> ('End of a Talk with a Jailer')

///

When you were young our national struggle for rights looked different. The world was a different place then. I was out of prison and actively working as a human rights lawyer with a dedicated team of people supporting the work. Gaza remained a prison for me through most of this time as I was unable to travel freely outside, with a few short exceptions. But yet, the possibility of change floated in the air. Now, I never invested too much in this possibility. The strategy of the occupation forces has always been clear. So, I could see a shift in methodology but not in their intentions: the total subjugation of our people. The occupation may have morphed from one shape to another but the essential structures that had been established, embedded through the philosophy of Zionism, meant that one person or another did not matter too much. Our bodies had felt the wrath of Rabin. While the world celebrates him as a man of peace we could feel the policy of 'broken bones': we knew our brothers had been lifted in helicopters and dropped out so they would become a burden to their family, incapable of working and stripped of their dignity. Of course we are ready to believe that any person can change. Even Rabin could change. As a human rights activist it is our role to see the essential humanity in every person, even our enemy, even the criminal. This is the challenge. But we could still feel the occupation and its crimes sitting on our chest and no amount of talking about peace could change that.

But despite this heavy weight we had a decision to make as activists because of the new reality presented to us. The Palestinian National Authority (PNA) was established in 1995 as the child of an agreement between the Palestinian Liberation Organisation and the Israeli government. Our family has deep links into the PLO, your uncles served on the council, we have always been linked into the organisation working to reform and improve it. We wanted to be supportive of the PLO but we knew immediately about the limits of the PNA. Although we were promised a fully fledged state by 4 May 1999 we could see the improbability of this. We could see the restrictions and limitations built into the structure of the PNA, its court system and its police and security apparatus. Our choice was to work against this flawed and limited offering or to work with it and build it up.

We chose this: on the one hand to work against the occupation with every peaceful and legitimate means at our disposal. We identified that the occupation was set to continue in all its legal and physical forms. As such we would treat the occupation as if the PNA did not exist. On the other hand we had a new quasi-state which we must accept. To do otherwise would be a betrayal of the opportunity and we preferred to remain loyal to the possibility of realising our national dreams. We wanted to build a culture of human rights within the Palestinian National Authority – we should treat the PNA as if the occupation did not exist, with full respect for the institution. We promoted high expectations of its capacity to respect the rights of people, even if it was operating under occupation. We did not want a stereotypical Arab state to be built – corruption, torture, restrictions on rights to organise politically and economic de-development. We wanted this to be the beginning of a process that would allow us the chance to breathe again. We believed we could build an oasis in the Arab world, a place where human rights, democracy and the rule of law could flourish.

Indeed to build an authority of this nature would be the best possible riposte to our enemies who claim a monopoly over human rights and democracy – even when they have no such monopoly. The creation of the PA was the creation of space. And so, the worst part of the occupation was lifted, very briefly, off our chests. I did not want to feel a stranger in my own land: our family has been here for hundreds of years. The PNA lifted the occupation from our chests. We took one deep breath. But when Arafat came to Gaza soon the PNA filled that space again. Now we had two stones sitting on us and we have barely been able to breathe since.

Initially, we began to observe deaths in custody in the Palestinian prisons which the new security forces had taken over from the Israelis. We expected these stories from the occupation but to have Palestinians killed by their own people: this was shocking. We spoke out against that and they were angry at the whole human rights community because of it. Secondly, they restricted the right to demonstrate and freedom of assembly. They created rules so that you need permission from the police – who, of course, refused to give permission. Then, in one night I remember they arrested one thousand three hundred Hamas and Popular Front for the Liberation of Palestine (PFLP) activists because they opposed the Oslo Accords. I knew many of these people – indeed I had been beside some of them in prison.

The next step was the creation of the state security courts, military-style kangaroo courts, which they claimed would be used only for collaborators. We came out very strongly against their establishment and I think this was the last straw for Arafat. That evening Eyad al Sarraj and I were both arrested. It was only for one and a half days but it was the worst period of my life. I knew then that anything I had dreamed for in the PNA was gone, if it ever existed.

Though the experience of this arrest was short I reached a difficult conclusion. You can be struggling all your life with people and they can betray your values. It hardened my resolve to seek justice for Palestinians in the outside world. I intensified my search for ways to work outside of the formal political process which had failed us time and again. At that time the legal instruments designed to protect civilians were undergoing a renaissance. The horrific events in Srebrenica and Rwanda led to the establishment of International Criminal Tribunals under the auspices of the United Nations. All of this was leading to an international movement for a court which would go beyond the politics of the situation and work independently on behalf of civilians. And this work by so many would eventually pay off.

DEFENDING HOPE

I think when the historians take a long view on our region they will see the turn of the millennium as among the most crucial periods of change in our struggle. Just one week after the enormous and successful UN Conference Against Racism in Durban, planes flew into the Twin Towers of New York. I knew and loved New York as a city I had lived in and where my dear friend Edward Said remained, at that time. Just months later the Rome Statute of the International Criminal Court came into effect and just over a year later Edward died of the cancer which had eaten his body. These events when placed together tell us something about the world. For me they drew the battle lines of the new world order. Edward famously said that in a choice between totalitarianism and imperialism one should choose neither. Meanwhile, President Bush was saying, 'You are with us or against us.' For me it was clear: I was against Bush, and against Bin Ladin and Netanyahu – all of whom wanted to organise the world around the rule of the jungle, not the rule of law. So, when Condeleezza Rice spoke about the 'birth pangs of a new Middle East' I knew our cause would be stillborn.

Watching the elections for the Palestinian Legislative Council in January 2006 only confirmed this perspective to me. Early that morning outside the blue and white United Nations school in Tel al Howa I watched as women, in *hijab* and in *niqab*, began to queue up to exercise their right to vote. Hours later they would come out of the polling station waving the black mark on their thumb (to indicate they had voted). People were proud because we held elections, despite the occupation. The international media spoke in glowing terms about the elections and even Jimmy Carter praised them as free and fair. You were only twelve at the time but I felt, for a brief moment, that this day would reshape the future available to you. This was something that I had worked for all my life. Your Mum had patiently nurtured you and your sister while I was in prison or out organising. She believed that a better future was possible for you both. This day was like a dream for us. But the prison maze is tricky to navigate: just as you turn one corner you realise that you have not reached the end.

As the results came in it became clear that Hamas were the victor. I have never been supportive of Hamas: neither their ideology nor their agenda. But politically speaking they are part of the Palestinian DNA and their victory should be respected as a principle of democracy. But we learned hard lessons in those days. As soon as Hamas' victory was declared Israel, and its international partners (the USA and the EU), immediately decided to boycott the Hamas government. This emboldened the banana republic officers of certain parts of the PNA who felt they, too, could boycott Hamas: and, so dividing the Palestinian political factions.

We learned the true test of a democracy is not the holding of elections but the smooth transition of power from one group to another. What prospects did we have when the whole of the world decided we did not deserve democracy? Electoral democracy is not mathematics, it is chemistry. When you enter the process you must be prepared to come out the other side with unexpected results. We Palestinians did not give the West and Israel the result they wanted. In return they betrayed our faith in a system that they had been demanding we should implement. They undermined the good work of the democratic forces across the whole region for generations to come.

DEFENDING **HOPE**

So, in the midst of three wars and ten years of siege, and ten years of feuds between Hamas and Fatah, I could feel how our national struggle was shrinking all the time. We no longer faced a struggle for the legitimate expression of our national rights but rather simply for some kind of normality. People want to live normal lives.

/ / /

But normality is a far cry for the people of Gaza. Over 1.7 million people live in the Gaza Strip, around half of them children under the age of eighteen. Seventy per cent of the population are refugees since the war of 1948. Gaza is one of the most densely populated places in the world, with the highest unemployment rate in the world and with little or no ability to move between Gaza and the West Bank or (via Egypt) to the outside world. Already people have suffered immensely – but insufficiently for Israel's soldier-politicians. But because of the election of Hamas and the disintegration in the Palestinian body politic Israel saw that our difficulty was their opportunity. Gaza was designated as having the status of 'Foreign Terrorist Entity'. This gave them carte blanche to behave towards Gaza as they saw fit and was the seed of the coming wars we would face. A siege was imposed on Gaza and the noose around people's necks tightened even further. Sometimes I hear Gaza being compared to a zoo but I know that the animals in any zoo are treated better than the civilians of Gaza.

Within a year the first of three deadly wars was unleashed against civilians inside Gaza. You lived alongside me for two of these wars, each one worse than its predecessor. No one in Gaza could feel safe with the bombardment coming from every direction, the constant flights of the drones and the F-16s. In fact no one in Gaza was safe. Our neighbourhood is rather middle class – our neighbours are doctors, or they work for international aid agencies and for governments. But our streets were not immune. The house shook all night from the bombing. The sound of gunfire and tank shells never ended. The smell of gunpowder and death permeated the air. Hospitals and schools were not immune to attack. As each night began we never knew if we would see the sun rise again.

The price of these wars was paid by the civilian population of Gaza. Civilians were in the eye of the storm. People were told by the army to flee: but flee to where? If each part of Gaza is under heavy bombardment where can people go? Israel applied the 'Dahiya doctrine' to the Gaza Strip – they destroyed whole neighbourhoods, turning them into rubble. No wonder that the war in 2014 resulted in the deaths of five hundred and fifty-six children.

The thousands of stories of civilian suffering from these wars are never far from my mind or heart. There is one that sits with me over and again: the Samouni family from the Zeitoun neighbourhood, east of Gaza city near the border with Israel. The extended family lived across the street from each other: kids, uncles, aunts and grandparents. On a normal day in Zeitoun the streets would be busy, though not packed like Gaza city itself. There might be a farmer bringing some sheep through the streets. Families would move strawberries to the market on the back of a donkey and cart. Maybe some of the young men would move around with small motorbikes, dust of the streets skipping from the tires as they turned corners. In Operation Cast Lead (2009) the Samouni family were trapped in their homes. Food supplies were running low. The Israeli military had surrounded the area and quickly taken control of it despite some small resistance from Islamic Jihad. In one house the soldiers kicked down the door and opened fire – they killed ten instantly. Inside another house one woman went into labour and her child was born the next morning. As the child was being born three of the men stepped outside to greet the morning and to smoke. They were immediately shot dead by the Israeli army. Inside the house people began to panic. From here, and another nearby home, the extended family decided to walk in a group out of their home to seek help in Gaza city. As they walked a sniper positioned on a rooftop shot one of the men in the legs and the women who tried to attend to him were told to stay back or they would also be shot. No ambulances were allowed in the area and three days later when one arrived they found him dead: he bled to death on the ground watching his family walk away from him.

Judge Richard Goldstone was appointed by the UN to investigate this war. It was later said that he 'retracted' his report. However, Goldstone simply said that he would take a different perspective with time and that he believed that the worst atrocity he investigated – that of the Samouni family – would be investigated by Israel.

As a lawyer your job is to examine the facts with a very open heart and mind. You have made a solemn commitment to upholding the rule of law over the rule of the jungle. Each case requires you to ask the difficult questions which the other side will pose to you.

'Was there fighting in the area?'

'Did this justify the military approach to breaking down the door and shooting before anything else?'

'Did the soldier who shot al Samouni know that he was unarmed, that he had been searched by other soldiers? Did he have a clear view or was it obscured by the smoke of the rubble?'

To establish these answers we had teams of researchers going from one member of the family to another. We took dozens of testimonies and cross-referenced each one endlessly. We double and triple checked the facts until we understood the best possible picture of the events. We even reported the death of an Islamic Jihad member in the area. Those who oppose us select this fact as proof that there was fighting and use it to justify the killings of civilians. But even the uncomfortable facts must be faced in the pursuit of truth. All the testimonies indicate that the fighting ended after about an hour and that the area was under full military control of the Israeli army by the time the killings started.

This is our mission: to look at facts, then the standards and to draw the conclusions. Our standard is the Fourth Geneva Convention whose purpose is to promote the protection of civilians during times of war. It is founded on two basic principles. First, armies must distinguish between combatants and civilians. Second, that anyone involved in fighting must attack only in a way that is proportionate to the threat faced by them. When we look at the established facts of the Samouni case it becomes impossible to deny the fact that these two basic principles of international law were violated deeply and significantly.

If this is true then Israel has the first responsibility for investigating the wrongdoing of its own soldiers. But as the legal representatives of sixty-seven members of the Samouni family we have been told that no one is to be held responsible for the death and destruction at the hands of the army.

In any rigorous investigation it is common practice, indeed an expected norm, that the people responsible for the alleged crime do not investigate themselves. We are all human: we have our biases and our judgements so we can not be expected to incriminate ourselves. For this reason an independent body should investigate such crimes. After all if the alleged criminal has done nothing wrong then they have nothing to fear from such an investigation. But Israel's decision to hold itself and its soldiers immune from any kind of prosecution for the Samouni family is an indication of its genuine unwillingness to face the reality of what the army is responsible for. Israel may have a very progressive high court on many issues but not on the question of Palestinians. Of the tens of thousands of cases which the Palestinian Centre for Human Rights took to the Israeli courts since 1995 only a small handful were successful.

Yet I have to place firm trust in the principles of the law – we have zero choice on this front. In prison I had learned that the pain must be deposited somewhere where it will not dominate your life but it can still be drawn upon to guide the search for justice: a kind of pain bank.

It is for this reason that we place our trust in the international system. Firstly, we have worked hard on universal jurisdiction and secondly with the International Criminal Court (ICC). The ICC was established after many years of campaigning by lawyers who wanted an impartial system to bring justice for victims of horrific crimes across the world. They wanted to free the suffering of victims from the hands of politicians and the power games which leave victims feeling double-victimised.

The ICC is a court for individuals – not for states. The ICC is not a Palestinian court: we did not set it up, nor did we ask for it. But we are now asking for it in order to seek justice at the international level. The case of the Palestinians is the greatest test yet for the ICC because it is the test of the court's true independence from political interference. When the court was created many on the political left criticised it as a tool of 'victor's justice'. On behalf of any victim of torture or extra-judicial execution by any state – whether Sudan or Yugoslavia – I reject this idea. But I do see that we Palestinians need the ICC yet they also need us. If we can not achieve justice at the ICC then it is a damning indictment of the court itself. The West is afraid because Israel is reminding them of crimes committed by American and British soldiers in Iraq or Afghanistan. But even in these countries there have been some investigations, some trials and some convictions. There is some sense of an independent investigatory authority. But Israel does not have an independent judicial arm capable of holding its military to account and so the ICC will play a significant role in bringing justice to the Palestinian victims.

We have brought three very clear cases to the ICC. One is on settlements, one is on the Gaza siege and the final one on the Gaza war. But of course the staff in the ICC continue to come under very serious political pressure – of that I am certain. Our first meeting with the ICC was with the Chief Prosecutor Luis

Moreno Ocampo. I liked him very much. But, ultimately, he was the one who pushed justice away by demanding that the Palestinians seek statehood in order to be allowed to bring cases to the court. This created a new roadblock and the issue once again became political. So we had to move towards achieving more international recognition for Palestinians at the UN – to achieve observer status. And of course the President of the PA (Mahmoud Abbas) resisted this. But he had nowhere to run during the 2014 Gaza war. I spoke to hundreds of media outlets: we were being bombed for fifty-one days and nights and he was doing nothing. So in the local and international media I called him a coward and I demanded that he intervene to protect his people. We also lobbied Hamas very strongly although we knew they would face the risk of prosecution because of some of the military actions they were taking. But in the end they acquiesced, saying that whatever they had to fear in terms of potential prosecution was nothing compared to what Israel would face. So, eventually Abbas moved to seek international recognition and here again we faced the ugliness of politics. Representatives of leading Western governments told the PLO that they could have international recognition of statehood so long as they promised to steer clear of the ICC. This ugly demand was a clear recognition of the fact that an Israeli war criminal could end up being prosecuted in the court.

I do not know what the future holds – but I do believe that we will see a day when an Israeli war criminal will sit in the dock in The Hague. Such an event will produce so many confused feelings for me. Firstly, I will be elated for the victims. They have waited too long for any sort of justice. It is a true and just demand of our people to see those responsible for the crimes against us brought to justice. The world should be aware that there is no holy blood and unholy blood, no holy suffering or unholy suffering. Every human body can suffer; every human body can bleed and even we Palestinians do bleed and we do suffer because we are a people. Those who have committed these crimes, and those who supported them, should have to face their shame.

Even so, I will have ambivalent feelings towards whoever is in the dock. I will be happy that they will face a free and fair trial from the most respected international judges of our time, more than Palestinians receive from Israel. I will be happy that they may begin to face the full weight and enormity of what they have done to our people. But I will be sad too. Sad because I know what it is to be a prisoner (even though I committed no crime). Life in prison is not an easy one.

Your great-grandfathers were landowners under the Ottoman Empire and became one of the significant families of the Gaza Strip. We are the children of this valley, the stones of this land that cannot easily be rooted out. We have been there since time began and we will continue to be there because we are on the correct side of history. They want us to give up, to leave and to lose hope.

Over many years my dreams have narrowed. Whereas once I dreamed of full statehood, now all I can dream is that ordinary people will be given a normal life to live, to trade, study, and travel freely inside and outside the Occupied Palestinian Territory. Although the extent of my demands have shrunk the strength of my idealism has not.

Now the search for justice is becoming yours. Idealism is a brightly burning fire – it is now your turn to carry it in pursuit of our dreams. May your struggle be victorious.

Yours with much love and full respect,

Raji

Afterword

Andrew Anderson

In June 2016 I visited Palestine and Israel. Over six days my colleague and I met with brilliant, tenacious, creative and brave human rights defenders who work non-violently on behalf of others in the brutally occupied West Bank or in an increasingly hostile Israel. We were not allowed access to meet with beleaguered human rights defenders in Gaza.

The work of these human rights defenders has never been easy. Today, it seems like the very right to peaceful protest or even dissent are in question. This was my fourth visit and each time it gets harder to sustain optimism in the face of a failed peace process and belligerent repression. A number of Palestinian citizens of Israel have recently been jailed for Facebook posts. We met in Haifa with Adalah, The Legal Centre for Arab Minority Rights In Israel, who say that over four hundred Palestinians have been arrested for 'incitement' linked to Facebook posts, including around two hundred and fifty who are citizens of Israel.

The situation for human rights defenders in the Occupied Palestinian Territory continues to be extremely difficult as they face threats, beatings, harassment, arbitrary detention, administrative detention and fabricated criminal charges. What was striking on this visit was the concerted nature of the attacks on human rights defenders working in Israel. Israeli extremist groups and government ministers seem to work in concert with each other.

We had the privilege of meeting the gentle Mohammed Khatib who led the creative protests which eventually resulted in the rerouting of the wall so the villagers of Bil'in can still access their land. But the villagers now live in the shadow of a huge illegal Israeli settlement.

The redoubtable Issa Amro showed us around the claustrophobic and repressive confines of the restricted H2 area of Hebron, where he and others sustain the struggle for Palestinian rights in spite of repeated detentions, assaults and threats. Imad Abu Shamsiyya showed us his house that was attacked after he filmed the extra-judicial execution of a wounded Palestinian youth who was lying on the ground after a failed knife attack. He also faces death threats and harassment because of his documentation of human rights violations.

The tenacious Nasser Nawaj'ah was displaced aged three from his village of Susya El-Kadis in the South Hebron hills in 1986, but refuses to be displaced from the surrounding lands. He lives with his family in a tent and continues to defend the land rights of his community and document the human rights abuses committed by settlers and the Israeli military. The temporary shelters of his people are repeatedly bulldozed by the Israeli military. An illegal settler outpost is untouched a few hundred metres away.

Israeli authorities and extremist Israeli groups work to defame, threaten and silence those who defend human rights. In recent years, this has included sustained and dishonest attacks on international funding of Palestinian and Israeli human rights organisations. It seems that the most vicious threats, defamation and attempted infiltration is targeted against those organisations working on international accountability for war crimes and crimes against humanity and those working to promote boycott, divestment and sanctions (BDS).

The Israeli organisation B'Tselem, which is one of the most respected and credible human rights organisations working

Afterword

anywhere in the world, has been targeted and its staff members have faced vile and threatening personal abuse. B'Tselem announced in 2016 that it will no longer refer complaints to the Israeli military law enforcement system because it is unwilling to continue to be complicit in a 'pretence'. Breaking the Silence, an organisation comprised of Israeli ex-soldiers that highlights abuses resulting from the occupation, has faced infiltration attempts and public attacks from right-wing media, government ministers and extremist groups. Prime Minister Benjamin Netanyahu condemned the group after an attempted sting by the extremist group Ad Kan, in spite of the fact that Breaking the Silence routinely ensures all the soldiers' testimonies it publishes are cleared by the military censor.

The Israeli government and extremist groups are also involved in efforts to criminalise non-violent efforts to promote international pressure against the fifty-year illegal occupation and aggressive settlement expansion. Denying Palestinians freedom of expression and the right to advocate for BDS are contrary to international human rights standards, and contribute to the continuous stripping away of peaceful tactics available to human rights defenders. It was very welcome upon returning to Ireland in 2016 to hear that the then Irish Foreign Minister Charlie Flanagan had joined his Dutch and Swedish counterparts in asserting that the right to advocate for BDS is a freedom of expression issue.

The courage and fundamental decency of the human rights defenders we met is one of the few signs of hope in a context that often provokes despair. That those who seek to use non-violent means to advance the cause of justice and full respect for the human rights of Palestinians and Israelis face threats, smears, infiltration and criminalisation is both sad and potentially very dangerous. The EU High Representative Federica Mogherini spoke recently of her opposition to boycotting Israel, but, as she has done before, she should continue to make clear the right of Palestinians and others to advocate non-violently in favour of a boycott, and the EU must visibly demonstrate their strong opposition to efforts to smear, criminalise and silence human rights defenders in Palestine and Israel.

Front Line Defenders works throughout the world to protect human rights defenders. Alongside those I mentioned above our cases have included some of the contributors to this book who have been imprisoned, tortured or otherwise faced serious risks to their personal safety because of the work they choose to do. Our advocacy work is always an uphill battle when faced with governments, like that of Israel, who use the justification of security to threaten and demonise those responsible for building respect across divides. But as one defender has told us 'it is never clear if the advocacy work has an impact on those governments. But you can be certain that it has an impact on me, on my friends and my family. Sometimes this is enough.'

It is not clear that this book will have an impact on the policies of the Israeli or Palestinian leaders. But if it has an impact on those defenders who have told their stories and on those readers who have engaged with the stories then perhaps this will be enough.

Andrew Anderson
Executive Director
Front Line Defenders, Dublin

Further Reading and Resources

Books

1. Michael Chabon, Ayelet Waldmanal, *Kingdom of Olives and Ash: Writers Confront the Occupation*, New York: Harper Collins, 2017.
2. Donald MacIntyre, *Gaza: Preparing for Dawn*, London: One World, 2017.
3. Jean-Pierre Filiu, *Gaza: A History*, London: Hurst & Co., 2014.
4. Edward Said, *The Question of Palestine*, New York: Vintage Books, 1992.
5. Richard Crowley, *No Man's Land: Dispatches from the Middle East*, Dublin: Liberties Press, 2007.
6. Laila El-Haddad, Maggie Schmitt, *The Gaza Kitchen*, Charlottesville, VA: Just World Books, 2016.
7. Vered Maimon, *Activestills: Photography as Protest in Palestine/Israel*, Vered & Grinbaum (eds), London: Pluto Press, 2016.
8. Mahmoud Darwish, *Unfortunately, It Was Paradise: Selected Poems*, California: University of California Press, 2003.

Online

1. Activestills; www.activestills.org.
2. BADIL, Palestinian Refugee Resource Centre; www.badil.org.
3. B'Tselem, the Israeli Information Centre for Human Rights in the Occupied Territories; www.btselem.org.
4. The Electronic Intifada; www.electronicintifada.net.
5. HaMoked, the Center for the Defence of the Individual; www.hamoked.org.
6. Haim Schwarczenberg; www.facebook.com/schwarczenberg.
7. Palestinian Centre for Human Rights; www.pchrgaza.org.
8. Women's Affairs Centre; www.site.wac.ps/en/.
9. Culture and Free Thought Association; www.web.cfta-ps.org.

Films

1. Emad Burnat, *5 Broken Cameras*, 2011.
2. Angela Godfrey-Goldstein, *High Hopes*, 2014.
3. Fida Qishta, *Where Should the Birds Fly*, 2013.
4. Yoav Gross, *Susya*, 2011.